FRENCH IN YOUR FACE!

The only book to match 1,001 smiles, frowns, and gestures to French expressions so you can learn to live the language!

LUC NISSET

New York Chicago San Francisco Lisbon London Madrid Mexico City
Milan New Delhi San Juan Seoul Singapore Sydney Toronto

Library of Congress Cataloging-in-Publication Data

Nisset, Luc.
    French in your face! / Luc Nisset.
      p. cm.
    Includes index.
    ISBN 0-07-143298-1
      1. French language—Textbooks for foreign speakers—English.   2. French language—
Social aspects.   3. French language—Spoken French.   I. Title.

    PC2129.E5N57   2006
    448.2'421—dc22   2006047030

À ma mère,
qui m'a donné, entre autres,
le goût des mots

5 6 7 8 9 10 DOC/DOC 1 6 5 4 3 2 1

ISBN-13: 978-0-07-143298-6
ISBN-10:   0-07-143298-1

English language editor: David Hayes
All illustrations by Luc Nisset
Interior design by Village Typographers, Inc.

Also in this series: Spanish in Your Face!

Also illustrated by Luc Nisset:
    101 French Idioms
    101 French Proverbs
    101 Spanish Idioms
    101 Spanish Proverbs
    101 Spanish Riddles

contents

"pre-face"

Let's face it: A face is worth a thousand words. It can reveal our character and signal our emotions and moods—even when we attempt to hide our feelings. You sometimes expect people to know how you feel just by looking at your face, which is convenient when, as often happens in France, your mouth is full! The messages that faces express are an essential ingredient of human interaction, but when we communicate in another language, this critical dimension is usually missing. In our effort to speak correctly and avoid mistakes, we adopt the self-conscious mentality of a dunce student, and we fail to notice and understand the facial expressions of the native speaker we are talking to.

French in Your Face! is designed to open up your receptivity to the other person's face! The French people are very emotional and sensitive: For them a wrong word is worth a thousand swords. But—and here's where this book comes in—they love to laugh! This book is your passport to communicating with these wonderful people; it links French terms, common expressions, idioms, colloquialisms, and even insults to the character, personality, mood, facial appearance, and gestures behind them. Enriching your knowledge of a language should be a rewarding source of pleasure. We hope you find this book and its illustrations to be funny, loud, opinionated, and, as the title suggests, *in your face!*

using this book

Just have fun! You can browse through the book, pausing where an illustration grabs your attention, or you can look up specific emotions or moods in the index or the detailed contents at the beginning of each unit, or you can take the lighthearted quizzes in each unit to pinpoint areas to focus on. Whichever way you use this book, enjoy it. It will enrich your French!

French in Your Face! has many unique features:

- Each of the 110 key terms in the first two units is accompanied by an illustration designed to provide context, reinforce meaning, and aid memorization.

- Captions provide English translations for the speech bubbles in the first unit and in the *gestures* section.

- Words that are synonymous or similar to each headword are listed, including adjectives, nouns, and verbs. Many of these are cognates or near-cognates of the English words, making them easier to learn.

- Related terms and expressions are listed to provide additional everyday vocabulary and commonly used phrases.

- Opposites are listed for some headwords. Note that in the sections *polar opposites* and *mood swings,* contrasting character types and emotions appear on facing pages.

- The symbol ◑ indicates colloquial terms or slang expressions that should be used only in appropriate situations. The French appreciate the risk you are taking in using slang, since it demonstrates your interest in their culture.

- Feminine forms and endings are indicated in parentheses.

abbreviations used in this book

adj	adjective
f	feminine
fpl	feminine plural
lit.	literally
m	masculine
m/f	masculine or feminine
mpl	masculine plural

character and personality

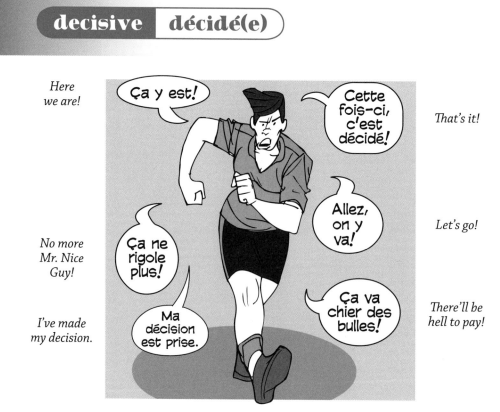

Here we are! — Ça y est!

That's it! — Cette fois-ci, c'est décidé!

No more Mr. Nice Guy! — Ça ne rigole plus!

Let's go! — Allez, on y va!

I've made my decision. — Ma décision est prise.

There'll be hell to pay! — Ça va chier des bulles!

synonyms and similar words

assuré(e) assured
buté(e) headstrong
certain(e) certain
confiant(e) confident
déterminé(e) determined
entêté(e) stubborn

ferme firm, assured
obstiné(e) pigheaded
opiniâtre persistent
résolu(e) resolute
tenace tenacious
volontaire determined

related terms and expressions

C'est un jusqu'au-boutiste. He's not a quitter.
Je n'en démords pas. I won't change my mind.
Je vais mener ce projet à bien, I'll do whatever it takes.
   coûte que coûte.
Ma décision est prise That's my decision,
   et je m'y tiens!   and I'm sticking to it!

faire un choix to make a choice
prendre le taureau par les cornes to grab the bull by the horns
prendre une résolution to take a stand

arrêté(e) fixed, settled
convenu(e) agreed
fixé(e) agreed
un arrêté a decree, statute

prêt(e) ready
réglé(e) settled
signé(e) signed

I'm not sure. I'm of two minds.

Je tergiverse.

Je n'arrive pas à me décider.

I can't decide.

I don't know what to think ... (lit., if it's lard or bacon).

Je ne sais pas si c'est du lard ou du cochon ...

Je me tâte.

I'm thinking about it.

J'hésite.

I'm undecided.

synonyms and similar words

ambigu(ë) ambivalent
brouillon(ne) disorganized, confused
confus(e) confused
désorienté(e) disoriented
dubitatif(-ive) dubious
embarrassé(e) confused, at a loss

flou(e) fuzzy
fuyant(e) fickle
hésitant(e) hesitant
incertain(e) unsure
perplexe bewildered, baffled
vague vague

related terms and expressions

Dans le doute, abstiens-toi.	When in doubt, don't do it.
Je suis dans l'expectative.	I'll wait and see.
Je tourne en rond.	I'm going around in circles.
Jean qui rit, Jean qui pleure.	He who laughs will soon cry.
Quelle girouette!	What a weathervane!

balancer to vacillate, waver
ballotter to flounder
flotter to fluctuate
peser le pour et le contre to weigh the pros and cons
une réponse de Normand a noncommittal reply

Wonderful!

I love it!

Super!

J'adore!

C'est le délire, c'est l'éclate!

Lui, c'est un vrai fan!

Tout feu, tout flamme!

It's terrific!
It's a blast!

The guy's a real fan!

On fire, real enthusiastic!

synonyms and similar words

dynamique dynamic
enflammé(e) inflamed, passionate
exalté(e) thrilled
fanatique fanatical
fervent(e) devoted
fou de crazy about
fougueux(-euse) enthusiastic

frénétique in a frenzy
impétueux(-euse) impetuous
lyrique lyrical
mystique mystical
passionné(e) passionate
ravi(e) overjoyed
surexcité(e) overexcited

related terms and expressions

avoir le feu sacré to burn with zeal
ne pas tarir d'éloges to be full of praise

◑ **accro** hooked (on)
dithyrambique ecstatic
emballé(e) excited

admirateur(-trice) *m/f* admirer
aficionado *m/f* devotee
disciple *m/f* disciple, follower
enragé(e) *m/f* fanatic;
  adj fanatical
envolée *f* **lyrique** lyrical flight
  of fancy

inconditionnel(le) wholehearted
partant(e) eager
possédé(e) possessed

◑ **fan/fana** *m/f* fan; **fana de** crazy
  about
fanatique *m/f* fanatic; *adj* fanatical
◑ **fondu(e)** *m/f* fanatic, freak
◑ **groupie** *f* groupie
◑ **mordu(e)** *m/f* fan, buff

Another party where people are having so much fun!

It's so depressing ...

I don't want to go!

Encore une de ces fêtes où tout le monde s'amuse comme des fous!

Ça me rend triste ...

Je ne veux pas y aller!

Mais, Josiane, c'est la soirée pour TON anniversaire!

Faut pas tout déprécier!

But, Josie, it's YOUR birthday party!

You can't put everything down!

synonyms and similar words

critique critical
détracteur(-trice) disparaging
dévalorisant(e) belittling

malheureux(-euse) unhappy
péjoratif(-ive) pejorative
pessimiste pessimistic

related terms and expressions

Tout de suite les mots qui blessent!   Hurtful words, right off the bat!

avoir mauvais esprit to be mean-spirited
casser la baraque to destroy someone's plans
censurer to censor
critiquer to criticize
dénigrer to denigrate
désapprouver to disapprove
juger to judge
lancer des piques to make cutting remarks
réfuter to refute

blessant(e) hurtful
cruel(le) cruel
cynique cynical

décourageant(e) discouraging
désabusé(e) disillusioned

gâte-sauce *f* party pooper
trouble-fête *m/f* killjoy, spoilsport

A computer doesn't make you clever or erudite.

It's curiosity, the desire to know ...

Ce n'est pas l'ordinateur qui rend intelligent ou cultivé.

C'est la curiosité, l'envie de savoir...

Nous on veut tout savoir, Mémé.

We wanna know everything, Grandma.

Et d'abord: où sont les mousses au chocolat?

First things first: where's the chocolate mousse?

synonyms and similar words

civilisé(e) civilized
cultivé(e) cultured, erudite
expert(e) expert
instruit(e) educated

lettré(e) well-read, learned
sage wise
savant(e) knowledgeable

related terms and expressions

C'est une encyclopédie vivante. She's a walking encyclopedia.
◐ **Elle en connaît un rayon!** She sure knows her stuff!
Elle en sait des choses. She knows a lot.
◐ **Elle est vachement rancardée!** She's wicked smart!

◐ **super calé(e)** supersmart

un cerveau a brain
◐ **une grosse tronche** a big brain
un puits de science a fount of knowledge

connaissance f understanding
conscience f awareness
culture f culture
érudition f erudition
génie m genius
sagesse f wisdom
le savoir knowledge

synonyms and similar words

analphabète illiterate
béotien(ne) uneducated
d'une ignorance crasse
  completely ignorant
élémentaire elementary, basic
fruste uncouth, unsophisticated
grossier(-ière) crude, coarse
ignare ignorant

illettré(e) illiterate
inculte uneducated
primaire crude
primitif(-ive) primitive
rudimentaire rudimentary
sans aucune culture uneducated
stérile void

related terms and expressions

◑ andouille f dumb-ass
âne m dunce
barbare m/f barbarian;
  adj barbaric
bête f fool; adj dumb
◑ con(ne) m/f stupid jerk;
  adj stupid
◑ connard m stupid bastard
◑ connasse f silly bitch

◑ couillon(ne) m/f asshole
◑ crétin(e) m/f moron; adj moronic
◑ débile m/f schmuck; adj dumb
◑ enflé(e) m/f numbskull
◑ enflure f numbskull
nul(le) m/f idiot
un vrai cancre a real dunce
◑ zozo m nincompoop

By meditating like that, he actually came up with the winning lottery number.

À force de méditer comme ça, un jour il a trouvé le numéro gagnant de la loterie...

Ça donne à réfléchir.

It makes you think.

synonyms and similar words

absorbé(e) absorbed
accaparé(e) preoccupied
attentif(-ive) attentive
méditatif(-ive) meditative
préoccupé(e) preoccupied
réfléchi(e) focused

related terms and expressions

Je suis accaparé(e) par ma profession.   I'm preoccupied with my job.

Je suis plongé(e) dans un abîme de réflexions.   I'm deep in thought.

abîmé(e)/perdu(e) dans ses pensées   lost in one's thoughts

What a scatterbrain!

I forgot my wallet!

I'm really just too disorganized!

My mind has gone blank!

I keep losing everything!

synonyms and similar words

absent(e) absent-minded	**étourdi(e)** thoughtless
brouillon(ne) messy	**inattentif(-ive)** inattentive
désordonné(e) disorganized	**lointain(e)** faraway
dissipé(e) wasted	**négligent(e)** negligent
écervelé(e) brain-dead	**rêveur(-euse)** spaced-out, dreamy

related terms and expressions

Ça rentre d'une oreille et ça ressort de l'autre.	It goes in one ear and out the other.
Elle est perdue dans ses pensées.	She's lost in her thoughts.
Il est dans la lune.	He has his head in the clouds.
Il n'a pas les pieds sur terre.	He doesn't have his feet firmly planted on the ground.
J'ai l'esprit ailleurs.	My mind is somewhere else.
J'ai la mémoire qui flanche.	My memory is failing me.

avoir des absences to draw a blank
écouter d'une oreille distraite to half-listen

◑ **cervelle** *f* **d'oiseau** birdbrain
mémoire *f* **sélective** selective memory
◑ **passoire** *f* memory sieve
◑ **tête** *f* **de linotte** scatterbrain
trou *m* **de mémoire** memory lapse

generous | **généreux(-euse)**

She has a heart of gold, she doesn't even count the money.

Elle est bonne comme le pain, elle donne sans compter.

Elle a le cœur sur la main.

She has a big heart.

synonyms and similar words

altruiste altruistic
bienfaisant(e) benevolent
bon(ne) good
charitable charitable
humain(e) humane, understanding

large generous
magnanime magnanimous
prodigue extravagant
royal(e) regal, princely

related terms and expressions

Elle a bon cœur.	She's good-hearted.
Elle donne aux pauvres.	She gives to the poor.
Elle fait l'aumône.	She gives to the poor.
Elle fait profiter de ses largesses.	She gives of her wealth.
Elle partage le gâteau.	She shares her assets.
Elle paye de sa personne.	She is personally committed.
Il donnerait sa chemise.	He would give the shirt off his back.
Qui donne aux pauvres, prête à Dieu.	Give to the poor, and you lay up a reward in heaven.
Un cœur grand comme ça!	A huge heart!
Une sainte, une bienfaitrice!	A saint, a benefactress!

mécène *m* sponsor, patron
philanthrope *m/f* philanthropist

Two euros! This skinflint only tipped me two euros!

Some customers are real rats!

Boy, can you be stingy! The tip is 15% of the check.

The quiche wasn't done.

synonyms and similar words

âpre au gain greedy
avaricieux(-euse) miserly
chiche niggardly
◑ **chien(ne)** mean, stingy
pingre *m/f* tightwad
radin(e) *m/f* cheapskate
◑ **rapiat** *m/f* stingy person

économe miserly, thrifty
◑ **écossais(e)** Scotch
mesquin(e) petty, mean
parcimonieux(-euse) parsimonious

related terms and expressions

◑ **avoir un oursin dans le porte-monnaie** to keep one's wallet closed
   (*lit.,* to have a sea urchin in one's wallet)
◑ **être constipé du morlingue** to be stingy (*lit.,* to have a constipated wallet)
◑ **être dur à la détente** to be slow to pay
être près de ses sous to be greedy
faire des économies de bouts de chandelle to save one's nickels and dimes
◑ **les lâcher avec un élastique** to be tight-fisted
lésiner to be cheap
◑ **mégoter** to be cheap
regarder à la dépense to hate to pay

◑ **grigou** *m* cheapskate
◑ **grippe-sou** *m* codger, penny-pincher
harpagon *m* Scrooge

You need a hand, ma'am?

Un p'tit coup de main, madame Pujol?

C'est pas de refus, mon petit Marc.

I won't say no, sweetie!

I like to help.

J'aime bien rendre service.

Tu es adorable!

You are so nice!

synonyms and similar words

altruiste altruistic
attentionné(e) attentive
bénévole benevolent
charitable charitable
empressé(e) overzealous

gentil(le) affectionate
obligeant(e) obliging
prévenant(e) considerate
secourable helpful
utile useful

related terms and expressions

Il faut s'entr'aider.   We should help each other.
Qui cherche à se rendre utile.   Always trying to be helpful.
Toujours prêt(e) à rendre service.   Always ready to help out.

dépanner to help out in a pinch
épauler to back up
prêter main forte to lend a strong hand
se serrer les coudes to close ranks in the face of adversity
sortir de la merde/mouise to get someone out of trouble
tendre une main secourable to reach out a helping hand
tirer d'affaire/d'embarras to save the day
tirer une épine du pied to get someone out of trouble
venir à la rescousse to come to the rescue
venir en aide to offer help

copinage _m_ help between friends
coup _m_ **de pouce** a little extra help

I couldn't care less! (lit., I'll whitewash my bellybutton with the brush of casualness!)

Alors ça, je m'en badigeonne le nombril avec le blaireau de la désinvolture!

Égoïste!

Quel jean-foutre!

How selfish!

What a lout!

Je m'en fiche.

I don't give a damn.

I don't give a rat's ass.

Je m'en contre-fous.

synonyms and similar words

apathique apathetic
blasé(e) blasé
cruel(le) cruel
désengagé(e) withdrawn
désinvolte casual
détaché(e) detached
dur(e) mean

égoïste selfish
fermé(e) totally uninterested
impassible impassive
imperturbable imperturbable
insensible insensitive
sans cœur heartless
stoïque stoic

related terms and expressions

Ça me laisse froid.	It leaves me cold.
Ça ne me fait ni chaud ni froid.	I could take it or leave it.
◑ Je m'en bats l'œil.	I don't give a rat's ass.
◑ Je m'en fous.	I don't give a damn.
Je m'en lave les mains.	I wash my hands of it.
Je m'en soucie comme de l'an 40.	I care as much as the year 40.
◑ Je m'en tamponne le coquillard.	I don't give a rat's ass.
◑ Je m'en tape.	I don't give a damn.
◑ J'en ai rien à branler.	I don't give a damn.
◑ J'en ai rien à cirer.	I don't give a rat's ass.
◑ J'en ai rien à foutre.	I don't give a damn.

◑ **je-m'en-foutiste** *m/f* person with a couldn't-care-less attitude

Hi, everybody!

Bonjour tout le monde!

N'hésitez pas à faire signe si vous avez besoin de moi!

Call if you need me!

Kisses, everybody!

Bises à tous!

synonyms and similar words

agréable agreeable
aimable likeable
attentionné(e) attentive
charmant(e) charming
délicat(e) thoughtful
doux (douce) sweet
gentillet(te) rather nice
gracieux(-euse) gracious
plaisant(e) pleasant
prévenant(e) considerate
sympathique nice
tranquille quiet

related terms and expressions

◑ **C'est un brave mec.**	He's a good guy.
C'est un chic type.	He's a nice guy.
C'est une chic fille.	She's a nice girl.
C'est une chouette nana.	She's a nice gal.
Oui, il est bien gentil.	Yes, he's very nice.
Vraiment adorable!	Just adorable!

What a shame! How cruel!

Thug!

Some people are sadistic.

Poor little thing!

Swine!

synonyms and similar words

blessant(e) hurtful
cruel(le) cruel
dur(e) coldhearted
haineux(-euse) spiteful
inhumain(e) inhumane
malveillant(e) malicious
mauvais(e) bad

pervers(e) perverted
sadique sadistic
sans cœur heartless
teigneux(-euse) cantankerous
○ **vache** mean, nasty
vilain(e) nasty, wicked

related terms and expressions

Il fait le mal pour le mal. He's being mean for the heck of it.
○ **Il m'a chié dans les bottes.** He did me dirty.
Il m'en a fait voir de toutes les couleurs. He really gave me a hard time.
Méchanceté gratuite. Being mean for the fun of it.

bête et méchant(e) mean and dumb
○ **dégueu/dégueulasse** dirty, mean
○ **vicieux(-euse)/vicelard(e)** vicious

coup *m* **fourré / crasse** *f* **/ sale coup** *m* **/ saleté** *f* **/ saloperie** *f* **/
tour** *m* **pendable / vacherie** *f* dirty trick

○ **chameau** *m* **/ chipie** *f* **/ vipère** *f*
hard ass
○ **chienne** *f* **/ garce** *f* **/ peau** *f* **de
vache / peste** *f* **/ salope** *f* bitch

mégère *f* shrew
○ **salaud/saligaud/salopard** *m* bastard
○ **vachard(e)** *m/f* mean person

I've got news for you: From now on we regroup, we grow up.

J'ai du nouveau pour vous: à partir de maintenant on se ressaisit, on mûrit.

Je veux sentir du respect et de la compréhension dans ce couple!

Le premier qui parle de divorce aura affaire à moi!

I want to see you show respect and understanding for one another!

The first one who brings up divorce will have to go through me!

synonyms and similar words

adulte adult
en avance advanced
posé(e) composed
précoce precocious
raisonnable reasonable

réfléchi(e) thoughtful
responsable responsible
sage wise
sérieux(-euse) serious

related terms and expressions

«Aux âmes bien nées, la valeur n'attend pas le nombre des années!» (*Le Cid* de Pierre Corneille)

"To those well born, bravery is not a matter of years."

C'est un(e) enfant prodige.

He's a child prodigy.

en avance sur son âge mature for his age

attention *f* attentiveness
circonspection *f* circumspection
discernement *m* judgment
intelligence *f* intelligence
maturité *f* maturity
prudence *f* caution
raison *f* reason
réflexion *f* thoughtfulness
sagesse *f* wisdom

Skip the math class! Bambi's playing in the Latin Quarter!

Shall we go?

Grow up, dude!

Does your mother know you're here?

You're so immature!

synonyms and similar words

adolescent(e) teenage
enfantin(e) babyish
futile superficial, shallow
immature immature
infantile infantile
irresponsable irresponsible
naïf(-ïve) naive

galopin *m* good-for-nothing
gamin(e) *m/f* kid
garnement *m* brat
○ **morveux(-euse)** *m/f* snotty little kid; *adj* snotty-nosed

related terms and expressions

○ **Qui c'est qui va changer tes langes?**   Who's going to change your diapers?

I know my place.

Moi je me tiens à ma place.

Je n'aime pas me mettre en avant.

I hate to brag.

I keep a low profile.

Je me fais toute petite.

I hate showing off.

Je n'aime pas me vanter.

Je suis comme mes revenus: modeste.

I'm like my income: modest.

synonyms and similar words

décent(e) decent
discret(-ète) discreet
effacé(e) self-effacing
humble humble
modéré(e) reasonable, moderate
pudique prudish
réservé(e) reserved
retenu(e) restrained
simple plain, simple
sobre serious, without excess

related terms and expressions

Chez elle c'est sans prétention. Her place is unpretentious.
Elle n'est pas frimeuse. She's not a show-off.
Elle ne fait pas de vagues. She doesn't make waves.

à la bonne franquette with a nice homey feeling
sans cérémonie without fanfare

I just bought two new villas in Cannes …

Je viens d'acquérir deux villas à Cannes...

Celui-là, avec son numéro de proprio, quel m'as-tu-vu!

Qu'est-ce qu'il frime, ce type!

This guy, with his big real estate mogul act, what a show-off!

What a show-off!

synonyms and similar words

bluffeur(-euse) *m/f* bluffer
cabotin(e) *m/f* ham
crâneur(-euse) *m/f* show-off
extraverti(e) *m/f* extrovert
fanfaron(ne) *m/f* braggart

m'as-tu-vu(e) *m/f* camera hog
poseur(-euse) *m/f* show-off
prétentieux(-euse) *m/f*
    conceited person
vantard(e) *m/f* boaster

related terms and expressions

C'est de la poudre aux yeux. It's all smoke and mirrors.
Il fait l'important. He is playing the VIP.
Il fait la roue. He's like a peacock.
Il joue les grands seigneurs. He's got a big-shot attitude.
Il la ramène sans arrêt. He sure brags a lot.
○ **Son truc c'est l'esbroufe.** He's good at showing off.

à faire son show to put on a show
avec ses grands airs with his big-shot attitude
en roulant des mécaniques trying to look big
pour épater la galerie to impress the crowd
toujours à faire le malin ou le mariole to always play the smart-ass or
    big shot
toujours en représentation always putting on a show

○ **l'épate** *f* smoke and mirrors   **le tralala** all fluff
○ **ses bobards** his lies/crap

She always looks on the bright side!

Elle voit toujours le côté positif des choses!

Elle dit que c'est gagné d'avance!

Elle envisage l'avenir sans crainte.

She says she has already won!

She has no fear of the future.

Of course, we're gonna make it!

Bien sûr qu'on va y arriver!

C'est dans la poche!

It's as good as done!

synonyms and similar words

comblé(e) overcome with joy
confiant(e) confident
content(e) glad
dynamique dynamic
encourageant(e) encouraging
euphorique euphoric

euphorisant(e) uplifting
lénifiant(e) soothing
positif(-ive) positive
rassurant(e) reassuring
sécurisant(e) comforting

apaiser to appease
calmer to calm someone down
rasséréner to calm someone down
rassurer to reassure
tranquilliser to put at ease

related terms and expressions

«**Tout va pour le mieux dans le meilleur des mondes.**»
(_Candide_ de Voltaire)

"Everything is for the best in the best of all worlds."

croire en sa bonne étoile to believe in one's lucky star
voir la vie en rose to see life through rose-colored glasses

synonyms and similar words

aigri(e) bitter
alarmiste alarmist
bilieux(-euse) irritable
cynique cynical
défaitiste defeatist
démoralisant(e) demoralizing

déprimé(e) depressed
inquiet(-ète) worried
maussade sullen
négatif(-ive) negative
râleur(-euse) crabby
sombre depressing

related terms and expressions

Ça laisse augurer le pire. — It's a bad omen.
Ce verre est à moitié vide, pas à moitié plein! — This glass is half empty, not half full!
Il craint le pire. — He fears the worst.
Il dramatise. — He's being dramatic.
Il se fait de la bile. — He's a worrier.

avoir le cafard to be down in the dumps

à-quoi-bonisme *m* what's-the-use attitude
sinistrose *f* grim attitude

This young man has manners.

Ce jeune homme connaît les usages.

Il est extrêmement bien élevé.

Un modèle de courtoisie!

He's very well behaved!

A model of courtesy!

Always so considerate and so proper!

Toujours si prévenant, si correct!

synonyms and similar words

affable good-natured
aimable likeable
attentionné(e) attentive
bien éduqué(e) well-educated
civil(e)/civilisé(e) civil

correct(e) appropriate
courtois(e) courteous
délicat(e) refined
distingué(e) sophisticated
empressé(e) courteous

related terms and expressions

attention *f* attentiveness
bienséance *f* etiquette
bonne éducation *f* good education
civilité *f* civility
correction *f* perfect manners
courtoisie *f* courtesy
distinction *f* refinement
égards *mpl* consideration, respect
galanterie *f* gallantry
politesse *f* politeness
protocole *m* protocol, formalities
savoir-vivre *m* manners, class

How rude!

He would walk all over you!

What a gross person!

Were you raised by wolves?

They think they're the only ones on earth!

He wouldn't even apologize!

Tell me if I'm in your way!

synonyms and similar words

effronté(e) shameless
grossier(-ère) crude
impertinent(e) impertinent
inconvenant(e) inappropriate
incorrect(e) improper
indélicat(e) unrefined
inélégant(e) inelegant
insolent(e) insolent
insultant(e) insulting
mal élevé(e) rude
malappris(e) loutish
malhonnête unseemly
malpoli(e) impolite
ordurier(-ère) filthy
rustre boorish

goujat *m* cad

related terms and expressions

gros mot *m* bad word
grossièreté *f* vulgarity
insulte *f* insult
mot *m* **grossier** swear word

I came to see you 20 years ago and you told me, "Life is a long, tranquil river."

J'étais venue vous voir il y a 20 ans et vous m'aviez dit: "La vie est un long fleuve tranquille."

Ça l'est toujours, mais c'est quand même mieux si vous avez la DSL.

That's still true, but it's even better if you have DSL.

synonyms and similar words

absolu(e) absolute
aigu(ë) sharp
avisé(e) wise
fin(e) clever
fort(e) strong
grand(e) great
grave serious
insondable deep
intense intense
lourd(e) heavy

métaphysique metaphysical
pénétrant(e) penetrating
perspicace perceptive
poussé(e) advanced
puissant(e) powerful
sagace shrewd
savant(e) knowledgeable
subtil(e) subtle
viscéral(e) visceral

related terms and expressions

C'est trop profond pour moi! Too deep for me!
«Paraître profond quand on "To appear profound when one is
n'est que vide et creux.» empty and shallow."
(Beaumarchais)

un esprit profond a sharp mind
le fruit de profondes réflexions the result of deep thinking
qui va au fond des choses that goes to the heart of things

Off to the hairdresser? Again! But you went there this morning.

Chez le coiffeur? Encore! Mais tu y es allée ce matin!

Je vais en voir un autre! J'ai besoin d'une seconde opinion. Je ne suis pas sûre de cette permanente!

I'm going to see another one! I need a second opinion. I'm not sure about this perm!

synonyms and similar words

creux(-euse) shallow
foufou (fofolle) goofy
frivole frivolous
futile superficial
illusoire unreal
immature immature
irréfléchi(e) thoughtless

léger(-ère) thoughtless
oiseux(-euse) idle
stérile unproductive
superflu(e) superfluous
vain(e) vain
versatile unpredictable
vide empty

◑ **cucul** *m/f* nitwit
sot(te) *m/f* idiot
trompeur(-euse) *m/f* cheater, phony

related terms and expressions

dire des lieux communs to speak in clichés
emprunter les sentiers battus to walk the traveled path
jeter de la poudre aux yeux to create smoke and mirrors
peigner la girafe to do busy work
tenir des propos en l'air to speak empty words

des balivernes *fpl* fiddle-faddle, nonsense
◑ **esbroufe** *f* showing off
façade *f* façade, appearance

◑ **frime** *f* showing off
lifting *m* face-lift
silicone *f* silicon
vernis *m* veneer

Relax, my old man. There are cold drinks and hammocks under the palm trees ...

Relaxez-vous, mon vieux. Il y a des boissons fraîches et des hamacs sous les palmiers...

*le FISC = France's counterpart of the U.S. Internal Revenue Service

synonyms and similar words

à l'aise at ease, comfortable
calme calm
cool cool
décontract laid-back
décontracté(e) relaxed
détendu(e) loose
doux (douce) sweet
flegmatique easy-going

indifférent(e) detached
paisible peaceful
peinard(e) laid-back
pépère comfy, at ease
placide placid
serein(e) serene
souple flexible
tranquille untroubled

related terms and expressions

Ça baigne. I'm on cloud nine.
On garde son sang-froid. Stay cool.
On se calme. Calm down.

être d'humeur égale to be even-tempered
rester Zen to stay Zen

d'un calme olympien calm like on Mount Olympus
jamais un mot plus haut que l'autre never upset
tranquille comme Baptiste quiet as a mouse (*lit.*, like Baptiste (the name commonly given to the simpleton in 18th-century farcical comedies))

She swallowed a clothes hanger.

That's her old-fashioned side showing.

Elle a avalé un cintre...

C'est son côté vieux-jeu.

C'est vrai qu'elle fait un peu collet-monté.

I agree, she does look a little uptight.

synonyms and similar words

affecté(e) affected
bloqué(e) blocked up
◑ **constipé(e)** constipated
empesé(e) rigid
engoncé(e) unbending
guindé(e) stuffy
pincé(e) hard-nosed

prude prudish
raide stiff
rigide rigid
sévère strict
strict(e) strict
tendu(e) tense

blocage *m* hang-up
défense *f* defense
résistance *f* resistance

related terms and expressions

Elle est amidonnée. She is really uptight.

rester sur son quant-à-soi to have a wait-and-see attitude

◑ **mal-baisée** needing it (sex) bad
raide comme un passe-lacet straight as a ramrod
sérieuse comme un pape serious as a priest

◑ **la bouche en cul de poule** lips like a chicken's ass

◑ **bégueule** *f* prude
◑ **un manche à balai** a broomstick
◑ **pète-sec** *m/f* / **rabat-joie** *m/f* killjoy

Your friend isn't very talkative.

Dis donc, ta copine, elle n'est pas très causante.

Elle ne parle pas pour ne rien dire, pas comme certains que je connais...

She doesn't just yak away like some people I know ...

synonyms and similar words

effacé(e) self-effacing
peu loquace quiet
réservé(e) reserved
silencieux(-euse) silent
taciturne taciturn

related terms and expressions

C'est à peine si on la remarque.	You barely notice her.
Elle la met en veilleuse.	She puts a lid on it.
Elle n'est pas du genre causant!	She's quiet—not the talkative kind!
Elle n'ouvre pas la bouche.	She keeps her mouth shut.
On ne l'entend pas.	We can't hear her.
Pas bavarde, dans son coin,	She's not talkative, staying over there,
à l'écart, elle s'exclue.	off by herself, keeping to herself.

I speak for everyone: SHUT YOUR MOUTH!

He can rattle on for hours!

He was vaccinated with a needle from a record player!

You're hogging the phone!

You can't turn off his jabber!

synonyms and similar words

causant(e) chatty
loquace loquacious

verbeux(-euse) verbose
volubile talkative

related terms and expressions

Et cancanier(-ère) avec ça!	What a gossip!
Il a un bagout!	He has the gift of gab!
◑ **On ne peut pas en placer une!**	You can't get a word in edgewise!
◑ **Quel baratineur(-euse)!**	What a smooth talker!
Quelle commère!	What a gossip!
Une commère/concierge/pipelette!	A gossip!

avoir de la répartie / du tac au tac to have a snappy reply
avoir la parole facile to have the gift of gab
◑ **faire un brin de causette** to have a little chat
◑ **tailler une bavette** to have a good chat

un phraseur / une phraseuse
  a wordsmith

un vrai moulin à paroles
  a real chatterbox

bavardage *m* yakking, gossip
◑ **bla-bla** *m* hogwash
conversation *f* à bâtons rompus
  banter

discussion *f* animée lively debate
◑ **parlotte** *f* chit-chat

self-confident | sûr(e) de soi

In life you have to push your way around!

Auntie's not afraid of anything!

Dans la vie, il faut savoir s'imposer!

Tatie n'a pas froid aux yeux!

Moi quand je serai grand, je veux être gonflé comme tante Irma!

When I grow up, I want balls like Aunt Irma!

Le culot, ça paie.

A lot of nerve always pays!

synonyms and similar words

assuré(e) assured, confident
audacieux(-euse) bold, audacious
certain(e) certain
confiant(e) self-confident
convaincu(e) convinced

fonceur(-euse) *m/f* go-getter; *adj* dynamic

related terms and expressions

○ **Elle en installe.** She makes an impression.
Elle fonce. She goes for it.

avoir _____ to have _____
  de l'aplomb confidence
  de l'assurance self-assurance
  de la confiance en soi self-confidence
  du cran nerve
  du culot gumption
culotté(e) smart-alecky
○ **gonflé(e)** cheeky, gutsy

I hate to be a bother. | Je ne voudrais surtout pas déranger. | Faites comme si je n'étais pas là. | *Don't mind me.*

synonyms and similar words

complexé(e) insecure
confus(e) confused
craintif(-ive) fearful
discret(-ète) discreet
gauche clumsy
gêné(e) embarrassed
godiche gauche
hésitant(e) hesitant
humble humble
indécis(e) indecisive

inhibé(e) inhibited
intimidé(e) intimidated
mal à l'aise awkward, ill at ease
modeste modest
peureux(-euse) bashful
renfermé(e) withdrawn
réservé(e) reserved
rougissant(e) blushing
timoré(e) frightened

related terms and expressions

Elle est dans ses petits souliers. She feels uncomfortable.
Elle monte dans le cerisier. She blushes. (*lit.,* She climbs a cherry tree.)

Elle ne sait pas où se mettre. She doesn't know where to hide.
Elle roule des yeux de merlan frit. She rolls her eyes (in fear) like a fish in the frying pan.

manquer de confiance en soi to lack self-confidence

frileux(-euse) insecure
pas tranquille tense
◑ **péteux(-euse)** ashamed, cowardly

I love people, what can I say?

As soon as I'm with company, I feel like they're family!

Moi, j'aime les gens, que voulez-vous !?

Dès que je suis avec quelqu'un, je me sens en famille!

C'est la crème des hommes!

He's the sweetest man!

So friendly!

Il est si convivial!

C'est ainsi que les humains devraient vivre!

This is the way people should live!

synonyms and similar words

agréable(e) agreeable
aimable likeable
convivial(e) friendly
drôle funny
facile easygoing
savoir-vivre *m* good manners

liant(e) gregarious
ouvert(e) open
poli(e) polite
sympathique nice

related terms and expressions

◑ **On est potes.**   We're buddies.

avoir le bras long / des relations / de l'entregent to have connections (in society)
avoir une vie sociale to have a social life
être connecté to be in the loop
être dans le coup to be with the in-crowd
grimper les échelons de la société to climb the social ladder
savoir vivre en société to live in high society

branché(e) plugged in, trendy
super sympa very nice, fun

bonne pâte *f* nice person
◑ **brave mec** *m* decent fellow

◑ **un super mec** a cool dude
◑ **une super nana** a cool gal

I don't like crowds.

At a party, I always keep to myself.

It's not like I'm shy or anything ...

I don't join in.

It's just that people scare me.

synonyms and similar words

antisocial(e) antisocial
asocial(e) antisocial; *m/f* social misfit
boudeur(-euse) sulky
circonspect(e) cautious
craintif(-ive) fearful
discret(-ète) discreet
froid(e) cold
glacial(e) icy

introverti(e) introverted
lointain(e) distant
marginal(e) marginal
misanthrope misanthropic
réservé(e) reserved
sauvage unsociable
secret(-ète) secretive
sévère harsh, severe

related terms and expressions

qui fait bande à part not joining in
qui s'exclue counting himself out

bernard-l'ermite *m* hermit crab
ermite *m* hermit
individualiste *m/f* individualist; *adj* individualistic
loup *m* **solitaire** lone wolf
non-conformiste *m/f* non-conformist; *adj* nonconformist
ours *m* grump
paria *m* outcast
◑ **pisse-froid** *m* killjoy

Let's see: vegetables, canned food, bread, kids, husband, car.

Récapitulons: légumes, conserves, baguette, enfants, mari, voiture.

Le compte y est.

Check.

synonyms and similar words

attentif(-ive) attentive
concentré(e) focused
méthodique methodical
ordonné(e) orderly, tidy
prêt(e) ready
prévoyant(e) farsighted
prudent(e) cautious
réfléchi(e) thoughtful
structuré(e) structured

agencer to direct
arranger to arrange
gérer to manage
préparer to prepare
prévoir to plan ahead
ranger to put away

related terms and expressions

garder la tête froide to keep a cool head
tout bien planifier to have a plan

qui ne laisse rien au hasard not leaving anything to chance
qui pense à tout thinking of everything

My mess, what mess? I know perfectly well where everything is!

It's somewhere in this clutter!

synonyms and similar words

bouleversé(e) jumbled
chambardé(e) turned upside down
déplacé(e) misplaced
dérangé(e) disordered
détraqué(e) unsettled
embrouillé(e) tangled up
mélangé(e) mixed up
renversé(e) turned upside down

related terms and expressions

◗ **foutre le bordel** to make a mess

◗ **bordélique** messy
pêle-mêle topsy-turvy

bazar *m* mess, clutter
capharnaüm *m* pandemonium, shambles
◗ **foutoir** *m* dump, chaos
◗ **merdier** *m* shitty mess
pagaille *f* mess, mayhem

synonyms and similar words

actif(-ive) active
assidu(e) hardworking
consciencieux(-euse) conscientious
bûcheur(-euse) *m/f* drudge; *adj* industrious

courageux(-euse) diligent
productif(-ive) productive
travailleur(-euse) hardworking

related terms and expressions

Au boulot! Let's go to work!
C'est un bourreau de travail. She's/He's a workaholic.
Elle abat de l'ouvrage. She's an eager beaver.
◔ **Elle bosse.** She slaves away.
◔ **Elle gagne sa croûte / sa pitance.** She earns her bread/chow.
◔ **Elle galère.** She slaves away.
◔ **Elle rame.** She works like a dog.
Elle s'investit. She really puts herself into her job.
◔ **Elle se casse le cul/tronc.** She works her ass off.
◔ **Elle se crève à la tâche.** She works herself to death.
Elle se donne de la peine. She is full of goodwill.
◔ **Elle se tue au boulot.** She kills herself working.
◔ **Elle sue sang et eau.** She sweats blood and tears.
Elle travaille d'arrache-pied. She works like a demon.
◔ **Elle va au charbon / à la mine.** She goes to work.

une vraie fourmi a real workhorse

Working is the way to health ...

Le travail c'est la santé...

rien faire c'est la conserver* ...

Doing nothing is the way to stay that way.

*French singer Henri Salvador

synonyms and similar words

bon(ne) à rien good-for-nothing
inactif(-ive) inactive

oisif(-ive) idle
paresseux(-euse) lazy

related terms and expressions

C'est un glandeur/branleur.	He's a bum.
C'est une feignasse.	He's a lazybones.
Il a un poil dans la main.	He's bone-lazy. (*lit.*, He has a hair growing in his hand.)
Il bulle, ce flemmard!	He bums around, the lazybones!
Il coince la bulle.	He just bums around.
Il n'en fout pas une rame.	He's a freaking bum.
Il ne fout rien de la journée.	He just farts around all day.
Il ne se tue pas au boulot.	He doesn't kill himself working.
Il se les roule.	He plays with his boogers.
Il se tourne les pouces.	He twiddles his thumbs.
La paresse est mère de tous les vices.	Laziness is the mother of all vices.
Partisan du moindre effort.	Welcome to the Lazy Club.

faire la grasse matinée to sleep late

cossard(e) *m/f* lazybones; *adj* bone-lazy

cul-de-plomb *m* lead-ass
traîne-lattes *mpl* lead shoes

What type of person are you? Depending on your answer to each of the following questions, you earn one or two points. Answer the questions and add up your score. If you need help, follow the cross-reference to the page(s) indicated.

1 • Vous voyez tout en noir (2) ou c'est gagné d'avance (1)? ☞ 20–21

2 • Êtes-vous très habile de vos dix doigts (1) ou pas dégourdi(e) pour deux sous? (2)? ☞ 46

3 • Votre ami gagne le loto! Vous êtes surexcité(e) (1) ou vous n'êtes qu'un sale rabat-joie (2)? ☞ 4–5

4 • Une copine à vous a des ennuis. Vous faites tout pour lui retirer une épine du pied (1) ou vous vous en tamponnez le coquillard (2)? ☞ 12–13

5 • Quelqu'un vous bouscule dans le métro. Vous vous mettez à râler tout de suite? Oui (2) ou non (1)? ☞ 41

6 • Il vous faut ouvrir le bureau demain matin, très tôt. On peut compter sur vous? Oui (1) ou non (2)? ☞ 67

7 • Un problème dans la cuisine juste avant la soirée! Vous réagissez de manière normale (1) ou pour vous c'est une vraie cata (2)? ☞ 62

8 • Êtes-vous bordélique (2) ou méthodique (1)? ☞ 34–35

9 • Dans un sauna, vous vous sentez un peu concon (2) ou parfaitement à l'aise (1)? ☞ 42

10 • Vous foncez dans le tas (1) ou vous manquez généralement de culot (2)? ☞ 30

11 • Un SDF (Sans Domicile Fixe) vous demande un peu de monnaie. Vous êtes constipé(e) du morlingue (2) ou vous vous montrez charitable (1)? ☞ 10-11

12 • Il faut se décider. Vous prenez le taureau par les cornes (1) ou vous tergiversez à n'en plus finir (2)? ☞ 2–3

13 • Êtes-vous du genre nul (2) ou êtes-vous un vrai puits de science (1)? ☞ 6–7

14 • Vous avez gagné un prix à un jeu télé. Vous ne vous sentez plus pisser (2) ou vous restez modeste (1)? ☞ 65

15 • Au bureau ou à l'école, vous êtes un bourreau de travail (1) ou vous n'en foutez pas une rame (2)? ☞ 36–37

16 • Dans une fête, êtes-vous plutôt du genre frimeur? Oui (2) ou non (1)? ☞ 19

17 • Êtes-vous très à cheval sur le protocole (1) ou êtes-vous plutôt sans-gêne (2)? ☞ 22–23

18 • Dans une soirée, êtes-vous du type liant (1) ou plutôt du genre qui fait bande à part? (2)? ☞ 32–33

19 • Acceptez-vous facilement de changer d'avis? Oui (1) ou non (2)? ☞ 45

20 • Un scandale a éclaté dans votre immeuble! Êtes-vous du genre discret (1) ou du genre concierge (2)? ☞ 28–29

To see how you did on the Personnalitest, turn to page 72.

He's a cuddle factory!

C'est une vraie usine à papouilles!

Il fait des mamours à n'en plus finir!

He just can't stop cuddling!

Il est super pote avec tout le monde!

He gets along with everybody!

synonyms and similar words

aimant(e) loving
câlin(e) cuddly
caressant(e) caressing
chaleureux(-euse) warm, friendly

doux (douce) sweet
expansif(-ive) effusive
◑ pote palsy-walsy, buddy-buddy
tendre tender

ami(e) intime *m/f* close friend
copain (copine) *m/f* pal
meilleur(e) ami(e) *m/f* best friend
petit(e) ami(e) *m/f* boyfriend (girlfriend)

câlin *m* cuddle
débordement *m* overflow, flood
effusion *f* effusion
élan *m* outpouring, surge
épanchement *m* display of affection
gros câlin lots of kisses
mamours *mpl* display of affection
tendresse *f* tenderness

related terms and expressions

Baiser de chien donne des puces.
(PROVERBE)

Don't trust someone who kisses you too much. (*lit.,* A dog's kisses bring fleas.)

Am I getting this glass of water today or tomorrow?

Alors c'est pour aujourd'hui ou pour demain, ce verre d'eau?

Incroyable, je peux crever de soif, tout le monde s'en fout ici!

Incredible! I could die of thirst here— they don't give a damn!

Famille de tarés!

Bunch of retards!

synonyms and similar words

acariâtre grumpy
acerbe caustic
chamailleur(-euse) quarrelsome
grincheux(-euse) grouchy
hargneux(-euse) churlish

râleur(-euse) crabby
revêche cranky
ronchon(ne) grumpy; *m/f* grouch
teigneux(-euse) cantankerous

bagarreur(-euse) *m/f* quarreler

querelleur(-euse) *m/f* squabbler

agresser verbalement to attack verbally
chercher la bagarre / le rapport de force to go looking for a fight

related terms and expressions

C'est une écorchée vive.
Elle aboie comme un roquet.
Elle démarre au quart de tour.
Elle est mordante.
Elle monte sur ses ergots.
Elle n'est pas à prendre avec des pincettes.

Elle prend la mouche.

She has thin skin.
She barks like a yappy little dog.
Anything will set her off.
She bites.
She is fast on the defensive.
Don't even try to grab her with tongs (because of her foul mood).
She flies off the handle easily.

aimable comme une porte de prison sweet like a jailhouse door
blessant(e) hurtful

mauvais poil *m* bad mood (*lit.*, bad hair)

mauvaise humeur *f* foul mood

Say, your mom looks a little constipated.

Dis donc, ta mère a l'air un peu constipé.

Elle bloque un peu quand je lui présente un jules.

She goes blank when I introduce a new boyfriend.

synonyms and similar words

emprunté(e) / endimanché(e)
clumsy, ill at ease

- **concon** *m/f* dumdum
- **cucu** *m/f* dope
  empoté *m/f* clumsy lout
- **godiche** *f* noodlehead
- **manche** *m* numskull
- **nunuche** *m/f* chump

related terms and expressions

avoir l'air d'une poule qui a trouvé un couteau to look like you're lost
(*lit.*, a chicken who found a knife)
avoir un blocage to blank out on something
être dans ses petits souliers to feel uncomfortable
(*lit.*, to be in small shoes)
ne pas savoir à quel saint se vouer to not know which way to turn
(*lit.*, which saint to pray to)
ne pas savoir sur quel pied danser to not know what to do
(*lit.*, which foot to dance on)

opposites

à l'aise comfortable
assuré(e) confident
décidé(e) decisive

libre free and easy
naturel(le) natural
relax relaxed

And then, blah blah blah ...

Et alors, bla bla, bla bla...

On s'emmerde à cent sous de l'heure!

Elle nous gonfle! Quelle enquiquineuse!

Y'a des longueurs!

C'est sans fin!

Elle bassine grave!

It's like watching paint dry!

She's a pain! What a bore!

It just goes on and on!

There's just no end to it!

She's a real pain in the ass!

synonyms and similar words

contrariant(e) frustrating
déplaisant(e) unpleasant
désagréable disagreeable
embêtant(e) irritating
fâcheux(-euse) annoying
fastidieux(-euse) dull
fatigant(e) tiring

gênant(e) annoying
laborieux(-euse) laborious
lancinant(e) throbbing
lassant(e) tedious
monotone boring
pesant(e) heavy, dull

related terms and expressions

◑ **C'est casse-couilles!** — It's a real pain in the ass!
◑ **Emmerdant comme la pluie!** — Boring as rain!
  On finit par se lasser. — Boring as hell.
◑ **On se fait chier/tartir comme des rats morts!** — We're bored stiff!
◑ **Quel raseur!** — What a drag!

assommant(e) incredibly boring
◑ **barbant(e)** boring
◑ **bassinant(e)** real boring
◑ **casse-pieds** boring; *m/f* pest
◑ **chiant(e)** freaking annoying
◑ **emmerdant(e)** deathly boring
◑ **emmerdeur(-euse)** pesky

enquiquinant(e) boring
◑ **gonflant(e)** mind-numbing
◑ **mortel(le)** dull
◑ **rasant(e)** boring
◑ **rasoir** boring
  soporifique sleep-inducing
◑ **soûlant(e)** tiresome

related terms and expressions

Tu es comme un éléphant dans un magasin de porcelaine!　You're like a bull in a china shop!

être gaffeur(-euse)　to always put one's foot in it

gauche　gawky
pataud(e)　clumsy

balourd(e) *m/f* dolt
gaffeur(-euse) *m/f* bungler
◑ **godiche** *m/f* noodlehead; *adj* dumb
◑ **gourde** *f* blockhead; *adj* stupid
lourdaud(e) *m/f* oaf; *adj* clumsy

opposites

être adroit(e) de ses mains　to be dexterous
être habile　to be handy

Let's make do with what we've got. (lit., Let's put the little dishes on the big ones.)

We'll come to an agreement.

I don't care either way.

It doesn't matter to me: six of one and half a dozen of the other.

I'm not all that difficult.

Live and let live.

Mettons les petits plats dans les grands.

Pour moi, c'est bonnet blanc et blanc bonnet.

On va se mettre d'accord.

Je ne suis pas compliquée.

Moi ça m'est égal.

Faut que tout le monde vive.

synonyms and similar words

accommodant(e) accommodating
arrangeant(e) accommodating
bienveillant(e) benevolent
commode convenient
complaisant(e) compliant
compréhensif(-ive) understanding
coulant(e) cool, easygoing
débonnaire good-natured
doux (douce) sweet
facile easygoing
flexible flexible
indulgent(e) indulgent
modéré(e) moderate
souple pliable

related terms and expressions

Coupons la poire en deux.   Let's meet halfway. (*lit.*, Let's cut the pear in half.)

Facile à vivre, pas la grosse tronche.   Easy to live with, not a big ego.

You think you're smarter than everybody else ...

Tu te crois toujours plus maligne que tout le monde...

Haha, c'est pas à un vieux singe qu'on apprend à faire des grimaces.

Ha ha, don't try to con a con artist.

Too clever for her own good.

Quand on fait trop le malin, il vous arrive des bricoles.

synonyms and similar words

astucieux(-euse) astute
débrouillard(e) resourceful
dégourdi(e) smart
déluré(e) quick-witted
éveillé(e) alert
fin(e) clever
futé(e) crafty
habile skillful

ingénieux(-euse) ingenious
intelligent(e) intelligent
malicieux(-euse) malicious
retors(e) twisted
roué(e) cunning
rusé(e) artful
sournois(e) sly

◑ **combinard(e)** *m/f* wheeler-dealer
◑ **démerdard(e)** *m/f* smart cookie
filou *m* rascal, crook
fin renard *m* sly customer

fine mouche *f* sly customer
◑ **mariole** *m* wise guy
◑ **roublard(e)** *m/f* crafty devil;
  adj cunning

À malin, malin et demi.   I'll outsmart you!
Rira bien qui rira le dernier.   I'll get the last laugh!

opposites

Elle est nœud-nœud.   She's dumb.
Elle n'est très fute-fute.   She's not the sharpest knife in the drawer.

◑ **bêta(sse)** dopey; *m/f* numskull
candide naive

niais(e) *m/f* fool

innocent(e) naive
nigaud(e) simple; *m/f* simpleton

Insane, isn't he?

I think this patient is nuts!

synonyms and similar words

aliéné(e) insane
anormal(e) abnormal
dément(e) demented
dérangé(e) deranged
déséquilibré(e) unbalanced
C'est fou. It's crazy.

détraqué(e) off one's rocker
insensé(e) insane
irrationnel(le) irrational
malade mental(e) *m/f*
  mentally ill person

related terms and expressions

❍ The following slang words mean "nuts": **allumé(e), atteint(e), barjo, branque, braque, brindezingue, cinglé(e), déjanté(e), dingue, fada, fêlé(e), fondu(e), frappadingue, frappé(e), givré(e), jeté(e), loufoque, maboul(e), marteau, pété(e), sinoque, siphonné(e), sonné(e), timbré(e), zinzin**

❍ **avoir des papillons sous l'abat-jour** to lose one's marbles
  (*lit.*, to have butterflies in the lampshade)

❍ **avoir une araignée dans le plafond** to have bats in the belfry
  perdre la boule ❍ / **la raison** / **la tête** / **le Nord** / **l'esprit** to lose one's mind

❍ **péter les plombs** to lose it (*lit.*, to blow a fuse)

opposites

calme / **équilibré(e)** / **judicieux(-euse)** / **normal(e)** / **raisonnable** /
  rationnel(le) / **sage** / **sensé(e)** normal, balanced, rational, wise

You can tell your boyfriend I'm watching him.

There's something going on!

Something's fishy!

There's a lizard!

I'm on my guard.

I smell a rat!

I sleep with one eye open.

Dis à ton petit ami que je l'ai à l'œil.

C'est louche!

Je fais gaffe.

Je ne dors que d'un œil.

Il y a anguille sous roche!

Y'a un lézard!

Ça sent l'amaque...

Tu vois le mal partout!

Tu te méfies de tout le monde.

T'es assez parano comme mec!

You see evil everywhere!

You don't trust anybody.

You're pretty paranoid!

synonyms and similar words

circonspect(e) circumspect
dubitatif(-ive) skeptical
inquiet(-ète) worried; *m/f* worrier
réservé(e) reserved
sceptique skeptical; *m/f* skeptic
soupçonneux(-euse) suspicious
suspicieux(-euse) suspicious

related terms and expressions

Chat échaudé craint l'eau froide.   Once bitten, twice shy.
Méfiance est mère de sûreté.   Caution is the mother of safety.
Méfiez-vous de l'eau qui dort.   Quiet waters run deep.

avoir des sentiments mitigés à son égard   to have mixed feelings about him/her

No argument!

Period!

The results are clear! (lit., *No photo required!*)

It's so obvious!

I won't let go!

You bet your life! (lit., *My hand to cut!*)

I'm 100 percent in favor!

I'm positive!

I'll fight to the death!

synonyms and similar words

absolu(e) absolute
autoritaire bossy
carré(e) straightforward
clair(e) clear
déterminé(e) determined
direct(e) direct
droit(e) straight
entêté(e) stubborn;
    m/f obstinate person
explicite explicit
ferme firm
formel(le) formal

impératif(-ive) imperative
impérieux(-euse) imperious
indiscutable indisputable
inébranlable unshakeable
inflexible inflexible
intraitable intractable
intransigeant(e) uncompromising
irréductible implacable
net(te) clear-cut, distinct
péremptoire peremptory
précis(e) accurate
tranchant(e) forthright, cutting

It's time for the mi-milk *of Mimi!* (lolo = milk)

C'est l'heure du lolo de Lola!

C'est un marginal!

C'est un personnage, un vrai numéro!

Le mec est grave.

He's a character, a real piece of work!

This guy's wacko.

What an oddball!

synonyms and similar words

anticonformiste nonconformist
○ **bargeot** bonkers
bizarre bizarre
○ **braque** crazy
○ **dingue** nuts; *m/f* nutcase
extravagant(e) eccentric
fantaisiste odd, eccentric
○ **farfelu(e)** scatterbrained
insolite strange
loufoque far-fetched; *m/f* screwball
original(e) eccentric; *m/f* oddball
singulier(-ère) weird
spécial(e) odd
○ **louftingue** *m* fruitcake

opposites

banal(e) banal
classique ordinary
○ **coincé(e)** uptight
commun(e) common
conformiste conformist

mesuré(e) moderate
ordinaire ordinary
raisonnable reasonable
sobre austere, low-key

You can do it, trust me!

Think so?

Sure!

She knows how to motivate her troops!

What a morale booster!

She's driven! What a boost!

synonyms and similar words

stimulant(e) stimulating
tonifiant(e) invigorating
valorisant(e) validating

déclic *m* trigger

related terms and expressions

dynamiser to energize
exhorter to exhort
inciter to incite
inspirer to inspire
motiver to motivate
remonter le moral à quelqu'un to boost someone's morale

opposites

démobilisateur(-trice) discouraging
démoralisant(e) demoralizing
démotivant(e) discouraging
déprimant(e) depressing
désespérant(e) despairing, hopeless

synonyms and similar words

calomnier to slander
dénigrer to denigrate
diffamer to slander
dire du mal to malign
discréditer to discredit
jaser to blab, gossip
médire to bad-mouth

bavardage *m* gossip
cancan *m* gossip
commérage *m* gossip
méchanceté *f* meanness
racontar *m* gossip
ragot *m* malicious gossip
rumeur *f* rumor

opposites

louer to praise
valoriser to validate
vanter to praise, vaunt

See here, the job was done according to regulations.

Voila, le travail a été fait conformément aux lois en vigueur.

Tu peux lui faire confiance: c'est un honnête homme.

Il est presque trop poli pour être honnête!

You can trust him: he's an honest man.

Almost too good to be true!

Mais je reconnais qu'il a l'air d'un brave mec, droit, franc du collier, intègre, loyal, responsable et scrupuleux.

But I see that he looks like a nice guy, straight, direct, upright, trustworthy, responsible, and scrupulous.

related terms and expressions

La décence, la droiture, la franchise et la fidélité sont des vertus rares de nos jours.

Decency, honesty, directness, and loyalty are scarce virtues nowadays.

Y'a plus de moralité.

There's no decency anymore.

opposites

déloyal(e) disloyal
faux (fausse) fake
félon(ne) felonious
fourbe untrustworthy
fumiste phony
malhonnête dishonest
perfide treacherous

canaille *f* scoundrel
crapule *f* scum
escroc *m* crook
fripouille *f* hoodlum
gangster *m* gangster
traître(sse) *m/f* traitor; *adj* treacherous
tricheur(-euse) *m/f* cheater
trompeur(-euse) *m/f* trickster
truand(e) *m/f* rascal, crook

I can't figure this guy out!

Je le calcule mal ce mec!

Il m'a l'air d'un cachottier.

He looks like he's hiding something.

He's a puzzle.

Il est trouble.

synonyms and similar words

ambigu(ë) ambiguous, enigmatic
dissimulateur(-trice) secretive
équivoque slippery
faux (fausse) phony
fourbe untrustworthy

hypocrite hypocritical;
  m/f hypocrite
menteur(-euse) lying; *m/f* liar
perfide sneaky
sournois(e) cagey

related terms and expressions

Avec ses airs de sainte nitouche on lui donnerait le Bon Dieu sans confession.

With her goody-goody looks, you could give her communion without confession.

avoir le regard fuyant to have darting eyes (insincere)
donner le change a quelqu'un to pull the wool over someone's eyes
faire semblant to make believe
jouer un double jeu to pull a double-cross
en cachette / en douce incognito, on the sly
duplicité *f* duplicity

opposites

direct(e) direct
droit(e) straight
franc(he) frank

intègre upright
loyal(e) loyal
sincère sincere

What a gross character!

You're never presentable!

Slovenly creep!

You depraved clod!

Fat disgusting jerk!

The look of this lazy bum kills me!

Quel grossier personnage!

T'es pas sortable!

Débraillé!

Espèce de clodo dévergondé !

Gros dégueulasse!

La dégaine de ce paumé me tue!

Papa, ton look SDF* dégage un max!

Tu vas pas encore nous faire un caca nerveux...

T'as qu'à amener le petit à des heures décentes!

You're not gonna lay a hormonal fit on me, are you?

Bring the kid at a decent hour!

Dad, your homeless look rules!

*SDF = sans domicile fixe = homeless

synonyms and similar words

choquant(e) shocking
contraire à la morale immoral
déplacé(e) inappropriate
impudique indecent, obscene
inconvenant(e) improper
incorrect(e) improper
obscène obscene

related terms and expressions

Quel manque de décence! What a lack of decency!
Quelle vulgarité! What vulgarity!
Sans vergogne! Shameless person!

mauvaises manières bad manners

opposites

approprié(e) appropriate
convenable proper
correct(e) proper, courteous
de bon goût in good taste

décent(e) decent
digne dignified
honnête moral
honorable honorable

There's nothing exciting about me.

Il n'y a rien d'intéressant à dire sur moi.

Passez plutôt à la page suivante.

Just turn the page.

synonyms and similar words

amorphe dull
banal(e) banal
commun(e) common
courant(e) common, ordinary
coutumier(-ère) average
○ **fadasse** drab
fade plain
falot(e) insignificant
inconsistant(e) characterless
insigniﬁant(e) unremarkable

insipide insipid
médiocre mediocre
modéré(e) average
moyen(ne) average
obscur(e) unknown
ordinaire ordinary
quelconque nondescript
terne dull
vague vague

related terms and expressions

être quelconque to be a dime a dozen

a petit budget low-budget

de second plan second-tier

gris(e) drab

incolore colorless

inodore et sans saveur odorless and tasteless

morne sullen

triste gloomy, dreary

bas *m* **de gamme** last of the lot, floor sample

Allow me to introduce myself: my name is Paul Marin.

Permettez-moi de me présenter: Paul Marin.

Je vous laisse faire connais-sance.

Enchanté. Christophe Brun.

I'll let you gentlemen get acquainted.

My pleasure. I'm Christopher Brown.

synonyms and similar words

charnière *f* go-between (*lit.,* hinge)
connexion *f* connection
contact *m* contact, connection
entremetteur(-euse) *m/f* go-between
lien *m* link

related terms and expressions

○ **Je vais te brancher avec cette nana!** I'll set you up with this gal!

○ **casser la baraque à/de quelqu'un** to ruin someone's reputation
faire l'entremetteur(-euse) pour quelqu'un to act as the go-between for someone
fusionner to merge
grouper to group
introduire quelqu'un dans l'affaire to bring someone into the picture
marier to marry
mettre quelqu'un en contact/rapport/relation to put someone in touch (with)
présenter to introduce
rassembler to bring together
relier to link up
rester en contact to keep in touch

par l'intermédiaire de / par l'entremise de through

These little darlings need to play.

They are most welcome.

Let them play—they don't bother me at all.

Ces chérubins ont besoin de s'amuser.

Ils sont les bienvenus, allez.

Vous êtes vraiment trop sympa.

Laissez-les jouer, ils ne me dérangent pas du tout.

Toujours arrangeante avec tout le monde.

You are so nice.

Always so easygoing with everyone.

synonyms and similar words

à la bonne franquette informal, casual
affectueux(-euse) loving
aimable amiable
amical(e) friendly
chaleureux(-euse) warm
compréhensif(-ive) understanding
○ **cool** cool, easygoing
cordial(e) cordial, warm
coulant(e) permissive
doux (douce) sweet
facile easygoing
indulgent(e) indulgent
pacifique peaceful
paisible gentle, easygoing
patient(e) patient
posé(e) calm
relax easygoing, laid-back
serein(e) serene
sympa pleasant
sympathique nice
tranquille quiet

A leader, a real chief. He's the boss.

He sure has charisma!

Un leader, un vrai chef. C'est le boss.

Il a un charisme!

C'est un meneur d'hommes, un rassembleur.

Ce type est un phare, une figure de proue!

He's a natural leader, a rallying point.

He's a beacon, an icon.

synonyms and similar words

gouvernant(e) governing
premier(-ère) de cordée first in line
responsable in charge

animateur(-trice) *m/f* leader,
  coordinator
◖ **le/la big boss** the bossman
◖ **le Big Chief** the head honcho
◖ **le/la boss** the boss
◖ **le cerveau** the brain, the boss
commandant(e) *m/f* commander
dirigeant(e) *m/f* leader
◖ **le/la dirlo** the big guy / big gal
employeur(-euse) *m/f* employer

entraîneur(-euse) *m/f* coach
guide *f* guide, spiritual guide
maître(sse) *m/f* chief, boss,
  teacher
patron(ne) *m/f* boss
supérieur(e) *m/f* superior
superviseur *m* supervisor
tête *f* head
◖ **la tronche** the brains

related terms and expressions

**«Ralliez-vous à mon panache
  blanc!»** (le roi Henri IV)

"Follow the white feather on my
  helmet!"

Wait, then the shrink says ...

Et alors, attendez, le psy lui dit...

Ce mec est trop marrant!

Il raconte bien les blagues.

This guy's so funny!

He knows how to tell a joke.

He's killing me!

Il me tue!

What a wild and crazy guy!

Quel déconneur!

He's a joke machine!

C'est une usine à gags!

synonyms and similar words

amuseur(-euse) *m/f* kidder, entertainer
animateur(-trice) *m/f* life of the party
blagueur(-euse) *m/f* jokester
◑ **charlot** *m* clown
comique *m/f* comedian
◑ **déconneur(-euse)** *m/f* joker, wacky person

farceur(-euse) *m/f* trickster
fêtard(e) *m/f* party animal
gai luron *m/f* a barrel of laughs
◑ **gugusse** *m* clown
joyeux drille *m* funny guy
oiseau *m* **de nuit** night owl
pantin *m* puppet
plaisantin *m* practical joker
◑ **rigolo(te)** *m/f* funny guy (gal)

related terms and expressions

C'est rigolo!	It's funny!
L'histoire se corse!	The plot thickens!
Tu connais la dernière?	Have you heard the latest joke?

◑ **déconner** to kid around
◑ **faire le clown** to act the clown
◑ **faire le con** to act up
◑ **faire le guignol** to clown around

◑ **faire le pitre** to clown around
◑ **faire le zouave** to goof off
◑ **lancer une vanne** to crack a joke

blague *f* / **boutade** *f* / **farce** *f* / **gag** *m* trick, practical joke, wisecrack
◑ **histoire** *f* **de cul** dirty joke

histoire *f* **drôle** funny story
jeu *m* **de mot** pun
poisson d'avril April fool, April fool's joke

Everything was against me, that's for sure …

Tout était contre moi, alors bien sûr…

On n'a aucun soutien de l'état …

I get no help from the government …

Everything's determined by age six.

Tout se joue avant 6 ans.

C'est la faute à Pas-de-chance…

Blame it on bad luck …

What a shame …

C'est dommage …

synonyms and similar words

aigri(e) embittered
amer(-ère) bitter
bon(ne) à rien good-for-nothing; *m/f* good-for-nothing
minable pathetic

échec *m* failure, defeat

◑ **nul(le)** worthless, hopeless
perdant(e) losing; *m/f* loser
recalé(e) flunked
vaincu(e) defeated

zéro *m* dead loss

related terms and expressions

échouer/rater to fail
faire banqueroute / déposer le bilan to go bankrupt
◑ **merder en beauté** to crash and burn
perdre to lose
◑ **prendre un râteau / une veste** to fail in seducing a woman
rater l'examen to flunk the test
◑ **rater le coche** to hit the dirt
◑ **rater son coup** to blow it
rentrer bredouille to come back empty-handed
◑ **se casser les dents / le nez / la gueule** to fall on one's face
◑ **se faire lourder/jeter/virer** to be kicked out, be dumped, get fired
◑ **se planter** to hit the deck
◑ **se prendre une gamelle** to fall flat on one's face
◑ **se ramasser en beauté** to screw up

C'est grave, gravissime! — *This is extremely serious!*

C'est une question de vie ou de mort! — *A matter of life and death!*

C'est la cata! — *It's a catastrophe!*

J'ai les boules! — *I'm scared to death!*

C'est trop flippant! — *This is way too scary!*

synonyms and similar words

démesuré(e) excessive
dramatique dramatic
énorme enormous
exagéré(e) exaggerated
excessif(-ive) excessive

extrême extreme
outrancier(-ère) extreme
pathétique pathetic
poignant(e) heartrending
théâtral(e) theatrical

related terms and expressions

◑ **Il en fait des tartines.**	He really piles it on.
◑ **Il en fait des tonnes.**	He lays it on thick.
◑ **Il en remet une louche.**	He's overdoing it. (*lit.*, He serves another ladle.)
◑ **Il est trop.**	He's too much.
◑ **Il pousse un peu.**	He lays it on thick.
Il va trop loin.	He's going too far.

opposites

mesuré(e) measured
modéré(e) reasonable
moyen(ne) average
normal(e) normal
pondéré(e) levelheaded

related terms and expressions

trouver un compromis to find a compromise
trouver un juste milieu to find a middle ground
trouver un terrain d'entente to find common ground

arbitre *m* referee
conciliateur(-trice) *m/f* mediator
entremetteur(-euse) *m/f* go-between
intermédiaire *m* intermediary
interprète *m/f* interpreter
négociateur(-trice) *m/f* negotiator

You've got lovely eyes, you know that?

I can see you coming from miles away!

This fellow hits on all the gals.

He's looking for adventure.

What a horny guy!

That flirt hit on me last week!

synonyms and similar words

un bourreau des cœurs a heartbreaker
un Casanova a Casanova
un(e) charmeur(-euse) a charmer
un coureur de jupons a skirt chaser
un Don Juan a Don Juan
un homme à femmes a womanizer
un tombeur a womanizer

C'est un(e) dragueur(-euse).	He's/She's a flirt (looking for a relationship or a fling).
C'est un(e) séducteur(-trice).	He's a seducer. / She's a seductress.

related terms and expressions

Il/Elle fait des ravages.	He/She can really sweep them off their feet.
Vous habitez chez vos parents?	Do you live with your parents?
Vous venez souvent ici?	Do you come here often?

What a show-off! And his kid, what a little punk!

Those two sure think highly of themselves!

Think they're God's gift!

They sure are showing off!

Pooh!

They're pretty arrogant.

synonyms and similar words

arrogant(e) arrogant
dédaigneux(-euse) disdainful
fier(-ère) proud
hautain(e) snobbish

méprisant(e) contemptuous
pédant(e) pedantic
présomptueux(-euse) presumptuous
supérieur(e) haughty

○ **bêcheur(-euse)** *m/f* stuck-up person; *adj* stuck-up
○ **crâneur(-euse)** *m/f* show-off; *adj* pretentious
○ **frimeur(-euse)** *m/f* show-off
○ **poseur(-euse)** *m/f* show-off; *adj* affected

related terms and expressions

Il ne se mouche pas du coude!	He thinks he's got class!
○ **Il ne se pas prend pour une merde!**	He thinks he's hot shit!
○ **Il ne se sent plus pisser.**	He's full of himself.
○ **Il pète plus haut que son cul!**	He farts higher than his asshole!
Il se croit sorti de la cuisse de Jupiter.	He thinks he's something special (*lit.*, he's come from Jupiter's thigh).
Le roi n'est pas son cousin!	He thinks he's tops! (*lit.*, The king is not his cousin.)

opposites

humble humble

modeste modest

My office is a bit small, but it has a view of my cars. They remind me that my business is rocking!

Mon bureau est un peu exigu, mais il donne sur mes voitures qui, elles, me rappellent que mes affaires n'ont jamais aussi bien marché.

synonyms and similar words

abondant(e) abundant
bienheureux(-euse) fortunate
chanceux(-euse) lucky
créatif(-ive) creative
fécond(e) productive, prolific
fertile productive
florissant(e) flourishing
fructueux(-euse) lucrative

créateur(-trice) *m/f* creator
producteur(-trice) *m/f* producer

généreux(-euse) generous, bountiful
heureux(-euse) happy
prodigue extravagant
productif(-ive) productive
prolifique prolific
riche wealthy

related terms and expressions

- **Je gagne un max de fric!** — I'm making big bucks!
- **Je me fais des couilles en or!** — I'm getting stinking rich!
- **être plein aux as** to be filthy rich
  vivre à l'aise to be well-off
  plein(e) plenty, full
  un maximum maximum, a lot

I can rely on her completely.

Is Gisèle trustworthy?

I would give her my keys without blinking.

Je me repose entièrement sur elle.

Gisèle est-elle une personne digne de confiance?

Je lui confie les clés les yeux fermés.

On peut compter sur elle! Elle ne vous laissera pas tomber.

Faites lui confiance!

C'est quelqu'un de sûr! On peu s'y fier.

Honnête et flexible, elle admet ses erreurs.

You can count on her! She'll never let you down.

You can rely on her!

She's dependable! You can trust her.

Honest and flexible, she's fully accountable.

synonyms and similar words

attentif(-ive) attentive
consciencieux(-euse) conscientious
crédible credible
minutieux(-euse) meticulous
ponctuel(le) punctual
sérieux(-euse) serious
travailleur(-euse) hardworking

opposites

On ne peut pas s'y fier.   He's unreliable.

dilettante amateur
fainéant(e) lazy
fantaisiste spacey
irresponsable irresponsible
○ **jean-foutre** unreliable guy, good-for-nothing
léger(-ère) inattentive
négligent(e) negligent

We all need some spice in our lives.

I respect that, but ...

On a tous besoin d'ajouter un peu de piquant dans sa vie...

Je respecte ça, mais...

Quoi, mon passe-temps devient trop envahissant?

Tu sais que mes hérissons t'adorent ...

What, is my hobby too intrusive?

You know that my porcupines love you ...

synonyms and similar words

attentif(-ive) attentive
attentionné(e) caring
empressé(e) overzealous

poli(e) polite
prévenant(e) considerate

attention *f* attention
considération *f* consideration
courtoisie *f* courtesy
égard *m* regard
prévenance *f* consideration

respect *m* respect
soin *m* care
sollicitude *f* solicitude, concern
souci *m* concern

related terms and expressions

être aux petits soins pour quelqu'un to attend to someone's every need
être très attentionné à l'égard de quelqu'un to attend to someone's every need
faire attention à to care for
prendre garde à to care for
prendre les gants to handle with kid gloves
songer à to care for

opposites

grossièreté *f* crudeness
impolitesse *f* rudeness
indifférence *f* indifference

manque *f* **de respect** disrespect
mépris *f* contempt
négligence *f* negligence

He loves me ... he loves me not.

It's not love, it's passion.

This guy makes me weak in the knees.

Stop coming on to me like that!

This isn't just sweet talk and a fling, right?

What ardor!

I love you, I adore you! Forever!

I'm crazy about you!

I've got you under my skin.

I'm nuts about you!

related terms and expressions

«**Chagrin d'amour dure toute la vie.**» (Florian)	"Heartbreak lasts forever."
«**Je t'aime aujourd'hui plus qu'hier et bien moins que demain.**» (Ronsart)	"I love you today more than yesterday and less than tomorrow."

avoir de l'adoration pour quelqu'un to adore someone
avoir de l'affection pour quelqu'un to have affection for someone
avoir de l'attachement pour quelqu'un to be committed to someone
avoir de la passion pour quelqu'un to feel passion for someone
avoir de la tendresse pour quelqu'un to have tender feelings for someone
avoir le coup de foudre to fall in love at first sight
être épris(e) to be enamored/smitten
être mordu(e) to be head over heels
tomber amoureux(-euse) to fall in love

éperdument amoureux(-euse) moonstruck, madly in love
fou amoureux (folle amoureuse) crazy/nuts about someone

un amoureux transi a bashful lover
crève-cœur *m* heartbreak

opposites

antipathie *f* / **aversion** *f* / **haine** *f* hatred, aversion

He's famous! He's on all the front pages!

This guy rocks!

Il est super connu, il fait la une de tous les journaux!

Ce mec cartonne en ce moment!

La presse en parle, il fait les gros titres!

The papers are all over him. He's making headlines!

All of Paris wants him!

Le Tout-Paris se le dispute!

Il a le vent en poupe!

He has the wind in his sails!

synonyms and similar words

acteur(-trice) *m/f* actor (actress)	**idole** *f* idol
célébrité *f* stardom, (a) celebrity	**monstre** *m* **sacré** superstar
étoile *f* star	**vedette** *f* star
célèbre famous	**en vogue** trendy
chéri(e) darling; *m/f* darling	**favori(te)** favorite
en vedette in the limelight	**«people»** celebrity; *mpl* celebrities

related terms and expressions

avoir la cote to be on the A-list, be popular
avoir le monde à ses pieds to be on top of the world
◔ **avoir le ticket avec quelqu'un** to be in good with someone
◔ **cartonner** to be a huge success
être au firmament to be at the pinnacle
être la coqueluche des Américains to be America's sweetheart
être le centre d'intérêt to be the center of attention
plaire/faire fureur to be all the rage

au sommet de la vague at the top of the heap
un succès fou very successful

la reine de la soirée the hit of the party
le point de mire de tous les regards the center of attention

I read my paper cover to cover every morning!

Je dévore mon canard tous les matins!

Il faut se tenir au courant de l'actualité.

You have to keep up with the news.

On ne me la fait pas!

You can't pull the wool over my eyes!

I like to stay informed, explore, consult the media, and check the facts.

J'aime me tenir informé, explorer, consulter les médias, faire des recherches.

Être branché, connecté, curieux, attentif, averti, avisé, renseigné!

One needs to be in the know, connected, interested, aware, informed, enlightened, and in the loop!

opposites

J'étais à cent lieues de me douter.	I was miles from having a clue!
⟲ Je suis largué(e).	I'm out of the loop.
Je tombe des nues.	I have no idea.
⟲ Là vous me trouez le cul!	I'm freaking stunned!
Première nouvelle!	First I've heard of it.

ignorant(e) ignorant
pas au courant unaware
sous-informé(e) ill-informed

Let's see how you did on the Personnalitest (pages 38–39) and what it reveals about your personality!

20–26 Bravo! Vous êtes une chouette personne que tout le monde se dispute! Pleine de gentillesse, d'attention et de considération pour autrui. Tout est bon chez vous, il n'y a rien à jeter! Mais il est temps de penser un peu moins aux autres et un peu plus à vous: charité bien ordonnée commence par soi-même!

27–33 Vous êtes un mélange équilibré d'égoïsme et de suffisance, avec pourtant assez de bons côtés pour vous faire des tonnes d'amis, vous fâcher avec régulièrement et... vous faire pardonner!

34–40 Mmmh... Vous n'êtes pas quelqu'un de facile à vivre! Aigri, démoralisant, coupeur de cheveux en quatre, même votre psy vous évite. Réapprenez à sourire aux autres: si vous ne le faites pas pour eux, faites-le pour vous!

moods, emotions, and attitudes

similar terms

assidu(e) assiduous
attentif(-ive) attentive
bien éveillé(e) wide-awake
prévenant(e) considerate of others
réfléchi(e) thoughtful
soigneux(-euse) careful
vigilant(e) vigilant

attention *f* attention
concentration *f* concentration
conscience *f* awareness
considération *f* consideration
empathie *f* empathy
intérêt *m* **soutenu** sustained interest
observateur *m* **attentif** close observer
soin *m* care
sollicitude *f* concern
vigilance *m* vigilance

common expressions

- **coller son nez sur un problème** to stick one's nose into a problem
  être à l'affût to be on the lookout
  être à l'écoute to be listening
  être absorbé(e) to be absorbed
- **faire gaffe** to stay alert, watch out (for)
  monter la garde to be on one's guard
  ouvrir l'œil to keep one's eyes open
  prêter une oreille attentive to lend an ear
  redoubler d'attention to be twice as attentive
  scruter to scrutinize
  se focaliser sur les points essentiels to focus on the essentials

Pfoulàlà!

similar terms

- **au bout du rouleau** totally beat
  exténué(e) exhausted
  vidé(e) de toute énergie wiped out

  assoupissement *m* drowsiness
  demi-sommeil *m* state of being half-asleep
  épuisement *m* exhaustion
  fatigue *f* fatigue
  lassitude *f* weariness
  perte *f* **d'attention** inattentiveness
  surmenage *m* overwork, overexertion
  torpeur *f* sleepiness

  être à bout de forces to be exhausted
  être à moitié endormi to be half-asleep

common expressions

- **Je m'écroule.**   I'm collapsing.
  Je n'arrive pas à garder les yeux   I can't keep my eyes open.
    ouverts.
  Je ne tiens plus debout.   I can't stay awake.
- **Je suis flagada!**   I'm dead tired!
- **Je suis HS (hors service)!**   I'm dead tired!
- **Je suis lessivé(e).**   I'm dead tired.
  Je tombe de sommeil.   I'm falling asleep.
- **Les jambes en coton, les pieds**   My legs are wobbly, my feet are clay!
    en compote!

  lutter contre le sommeil to fight off sleep

- **à plat(e)** whipped, run down
- **crevé(e)** really tired
  éreinté(e) exhausted
- **flapi(e)** wiped out
  mort(e) de fatigue dead tired
- **moulu(e)** worn out
- **pompé(e)** bushed
- **vanné(e)** dead tired

Zen

similar terms

d'un calme olympien with godly calm
décontracté(e) at ease
détendu(e) relaxed
flegmatique impassive
maître(sse) (de soi) self-controlled
paisible at peace
posé(e) poised
réfléchi(e) thoughtful
serein(e) serene
tranquille peaceful, tranquil

air *m* **calme / caractère** *m* **calme /
    humeur** *f* **calme** calm attitude/mood
certitude *f* certainty
confiance *f* confidence
paix *f* **intérieure** inner peace
quiétude *f* tranquility
repos *m* **de l'esprit / de l'âme** peace of mind
sang-froid *m* cool under pressure
sérénité *f* serenity
tranquillité *f* calm, peace

common expressions

Il faut rester maître(sse) de soi. You need to keep your cool.
Inutile de s'énerver. No need to get upset.
◑ **On se calme.** Calm down.
◑ **Zen, le mec (la nana).** Zen, the dude (the gal).

contrôler ses émotions to control his/her emotions

◑ **relax** relaxed
◑ **super cool/relax** totally cool

Aïe aïe!

similar terms

oppressé(e) stressed
tendu(e) tense
tourmenté(e) worried

avoir la gorge serrée to have a lump in one's throat
avoir le cœur serré to feel heartache
éprouver un sentiment d'insécurité to feel insecure

frayeur *f* fright
inquiétude *f* worry
peur *f* fear
tension *f* tension
trac *m* stage fright

common expressions

J'ai un de ces tracs!	I'm very scared!
◑ **Je craque!**	I'm having a breakdown!
◑ **Je flippe!**	I'm stressed!
Je me ronge les ongles.	I'm biting my nails.
Je me sens crispé(e).	I'm on edge.
Je me sens nerveux(-euse).	I'm nervous.
◑ **Je me sens parano.**	I'm paranoid.
Je ne suis pas tranquille.	I'm not at all relaxed.
Je suis dans un état de nervosité!	I'm a nervous wreck.

pas à prendre avec des pincettes to be very nervous

Yeah!

similar terms

allègre lively
content(e) glad
enjoué(e) playful
jovial(e) merry
joyeux(-euse) joyful
léger(e) light
réjoui(e) cheerful

esprit *m* spirit
fantaisie *f* whim
gaieté *f* cheerfulness
hilarité *f* hilarity
humour *m* humor
plaisanterie *f* joke

common expressions

Allons-y gaiement!	Let's go merrily along!
Bonjour les hirondelles!	Hello, pretty swallows!
Ça baigne!	Everything is going so well!
J'ai le cœur léger!	I'm lighthearted!
Je jubile!	I'm elated!
Je plane!	I'm floating on air!
Je rayonne!	I'm beaming!
Je suis d'humeur badine!	I'm in a fun-loving mood!
Je suis d'humeur primesautière!	I'm in a carefree mood!
Je suis gai(e) comme un pinson!	I'm happy as a lark!
La vie est belle!	Isn't life beautiful!

Beuh.

similar terms

affligé(e) afflicted
chagriné(e) saddened
déprimé(e) depressed
maussade dull
morose morose
sombre grim

chagrin *m* sorrow
dépression *f* depression
détresse *f* distress
la mort *f* **dans l'âme** (with) a heavy heart
peine *f* sadness
spleen *m* despondency

common expressions

◑ **C'est la super déprime!**   It's the pits!
◑ **J'ai un de ces cafards!**   I'm down in the dumps.
  J'en ai gros sur le cœur.   I'm very upset.
  Je broye du noir.   I'm feeling blue.
  Je suis au creux de la vague.   I'm at rock bottom.
  Je suis triste à pleurer.   I'm so sad I could cry.

être comme une âme en peine to be a soul in torment

au 36ème dessous at rock bottom
au bord des larmes on the verge of tears

le chevalier à la triste figure (Don Quichotte) the knight with the sad face
  (Don Quixote)

Ça va?

similar terms

accommodant(e) accommodating
accueillant(e) welcoming
agréable agreeable
aimable likeable
attentionné(e) caring
bienveillant(e) benevolent
chaleureux(-euse) warm
cordial(e) friendly
facile easygoing
gentil(le) nice
gracieux(-euse) gracious
ouvert(e) open
poli(e) polite
sociable sociable
souriant(e) smiling
spontané(e) spontaneous
sympathique nice, pleasant

amabilité *f* pleasantness
attention *f* attentiveness
civilité *f* courtesy
politesse *f* politeness

common expressions

C'est la crème des hommes! — He's the sweetest man!
◑ **C'est un vrai pote.** — He's a real pal.
Il n'a que des amis. — He has no enemies.
Toujours là pour les copains! — Always there for his friends!
Toujours un mot gentil! — Always with a kind word!

◑ **jamais de chichis** never fussy

le regard franc a sincere look

similar terms

acariâtre cantankerous
acerbe caustic
antipathique unpleasant
belliqueux(-euse) bellicose
bileux(-euse) irritable
désagréable unpleasant
grincheux(-euse) grumpy
haineux(-euse) hateful
hostile hostile
méchant(e) mean
querelleur(-euse) quarrelsome
rébarbatif(-ive) repulsive
vindicatif(-ive) vindictive

animosité *f* animosity
haine *f* hatred
hostilité *f* hostility
répulsion *f* feeling of repulsion

détester to despise
exécrer to loathe

GRR.

common expressions

◐ **Elle a trop la haine.**	She has too much hatred.
◐ **Elle gueule après tout le monde.**	She yells at everybody.
Elle ne peut voir personne en peinture!	She can't stand anybody!
Elle vous mordrait.	She would bite you.
◐ **Je l'ai dans le nez!**	I've had her up to here (*lit.*, in the nose)!
Je la déteste!	I can't stand her!
On est à couteaux tirés!	We're close to strangling (*lit.*, throwing knives at) each other!
Quel sale caractère!	What a foul temper!
Sa vue m'insupporte!	I can't stand the sight of her!

similar terms

**Pour faire partie des «honnêtes gens»,
il faut être _____** To be one of the
good guys, you've got to be _____

aimant(e) loving
bien sous tous les rapports good in
every respect
civil(e) civilized
croyant(e) faithful
droit(e) upstanding
drôle funny
fidèle faithful
généreux(-euse) generous
gentil(le) kind
humain(e) humane
instruit(e) educated
intègre upright
juste fair
loyal(e) loyal
modeste modest
moral(e) moral
normal(e) normal
patriote patriotic
productif(-ive) productive
respecté(e) de tous respected in the
community
scrupuleux(-euse) scrupulous
sensible sensitive
serviable helpful
sincère sincere

common expressions

C'est la crème des hommes/femmes. He/She is the perfect guy/gal.
C'est un amour. He/She is a peach.
C'est un bon p'tit gars. He's a good li'l guy.

bon vivant fun-loving
bon(ne) comme le pain good as gold
bosseur(-euse) hardworking

le bon bougre a good sort
les Bons *mpl* the good guys
brave garçon *m* nice young man
◑ **un brave mec** a decent guy
les braves gens the good folks
un chic type nice guy, good Joe

facile à vivre easygoing
pas fier (fière) unpretentious
sympa friendly

une femme bien a good woman
les mains propres a clean past
◑ **nana** *f* **sympa** nice gal
pas le mauvais cheval not a bad
guy
la tête haute beyond reproach

GRRR!

similar terms

bête et méchant(e) dumb and mean
brutal(e) violent, brutal
cruel(le) cruel
égoïste selfish
inhumain(e) inhumane
malhonnête dishonest
malveillant(e) malevolent
mauvais(e) bad
obsédé(e) obsessed
sanguinaire bloodthirsty
sans-cœur heartless
violent(e) violent

bandit *m* gangster
casseur *m* thug
délateur(-trice) *m/f* squealer, informer
escroc *m* crook
exploiteur(-euse) *m/f* user, exploiter
oppresseur *m* oppressor
pervers *m/f* pervert
prédateur(-trice) *m/f* predator
profiteur(-euse) *m/f* opportunist

proxénète *m* pimp
raciste *m/f* racist
sadique *m/f* sadist
terroriste *m/f* terrorist
tortionnaire *m/f* torturer
trafiquant(e) *m/f* trafficker
tueur(-euse) *m/f* murderer
tyran *m* tyrant
violeur *m* rapist
voleur(-euse) *m/f* thief

common expressions

◑ **Ce mec est un empaffé!** This guy's a jerk!
◑ **Ce mec est une vache!** This guy's a mean son of a gun!
◑ **Ce mec est une vraie pute!** This guy's a real scumbag!

◑ **dégueulasse** disgusting
◑ **pourri(e)** rotten

◑ **affameur(-euse)** *m/f* stingy boss
◑ **une bande d'enfoirés** a bunch of bad asses
◑ **un beau panier de crabes** a bunch of crooks
◑ **chauffard** *m* reckless driver
◑ **clodo** *m/f* bum
◑ **cochon(ne)** *m/f* lecher, pig
◑ **couille molle** *f* wimp
◑ **crapule** *f* scum
◑ **enfoiré(e)** *m/f* dumb-ass
◑ **fumier** *m* turd
◑ **glandeur(-euse)** *m/f* lazy bum

◑ **harcèleur(-euse)** *m/f* harasser
◑ **les Méchants** *mpl* the bad guys, baddies
◑ **mouchard(e)** *m/f* informer
◑ **pue de la gueule** *m* bad-breathed freak
◑ **requin** *m* shark
◑ **salaud** *m* / **salopard** *m* bastard
◑ **saligaud** *m* dirty pig
◑ **salope** *f* bitch
◑ **sangsue** *f* leech
◑ **traîne-lattes** *f* bum

Rââh!

similar terms

béat(e) blissfully happy
bienheureux(-euse) happy
chanceux(-euse) lucky
comblé(e) sated
content(e) glad
enjoué(e) playful
fortuné(e) fortunate
gai(e) merry
joyeux(-euse) joyful
radieux(-euse) beaming
ravi(e) delighted
satisfait(e) satisfied
serein(e) serene
souriant(e) cheerful

enchantement *m* enchantment
euphorie *f* euphoria
félicité *f* bliss
joie *f* joy
liesse *f* jubilation
plaisir *m* pleasure
ravissement *m* rapture
rayonnement *m* radiance

common expressions

◑ À l'aise, Blaise!	At ease, Louise!
◑ Ça baigne dans l'huile!	Everything is going smoothly!
◑ Cool!	Cool!
Heureux au jeu, malheureux en amour.	Lucky at gambling, unlucky at love.
◑ J'ai la banane.	I have a huge smile.
Je bois du petit lait.	I feel terrific.
Je ne touche pas terre.	I'm walking on air.
◑ Je pète le feu.	I'm full of beans/energy. (*lit.*, I'm farting fire.)
Je plane.	I'm floating on air.
Je suis aux anges / au 7ème ciel.	I'm on cloud nine / in seventh heaven.
Je suis bien dans ma peau!	I feel great about myself.
Je suis super bien luné(e).	I'm in a great mood.
être heureux comme un roi/pape	to be happy as a king/pope

Houlà!

similar terms

affligé(e) afflicted
éprouvé(e) stricken
infortuné(e) unfortunate
misérable miserable
pathétique pathetic
pauvre poor
piteux(-euse) pitiful
pitoyable pitiful
triste sad

accident *m* accident
adversité *f* adversity
chagrin *m* sorrow
coup *m* **dur** setback
désastre *m* disaster
deuil *m* grief, mourning
drame *m* tragedy
échec *m* failure
épreuve *f* hardship
fatalité *f* casualty, accident
fléau *m* blight
infortune *f* misfortune

malchance *f* bad luck
malheur *m* misfortune
misère *f* misery
peine *f* sorrow, pain
perte *f* loss
revers *f* reversal (of fortune), setback
ruine *f* ruin
tragédie *f* tragedy

common expressions

À quelque chose malheur est bon.   Every cloud has a silver lining.
Un malheur ne vient jamais seul.   It never rains but it pours.

broyer du noir to brood
vivre un mélo(drame) to be like a bad soap opera

◑ **au bout du rouleau** at one's wit's end
catastrophé(e) devastated
déchiré(e) torn apart
malheureux(-euse) comme les pierres as miserable as sin

◑ **la cata** catastrophe
◑ **chienne** *f* **de vie** a bitch of a life
◑ **la mafre** no luck, dumb luck
le mauvais œil bad omen
◑ **pas** *m* **de pot** no luck, dumb luck
◑ **la poisse** bad luck
◑ **la scoumoune** bad luck
◑ **une vie de chien** a dog's life

Vas-y!

similar terms

dithyrambique ecstatic, full of praise
dynamisant(e) energizing
encourageant(e) encouraging
positif(-ive) positive
réconfortant(e) comforting, cheering
tonique boosting
valorisant(e) validating

applaudissement *m* applause
approbation *f* approval
appui *m* support
compliment *m* compliment
éloge *m* praise
félicitation *f* congratulations
hommage *m* tribute
louange *m* praise
soutien *m* support

faire l'apologie to praise

common expressions

Bravo! Excellent! Courage! — Bravo! Excellent! Keep going!
Elle ne tarit pas d'éloges. — She is full of praise.
Tu peux le faire! Fais-toi confiance! — You can do it! Believe in yourself!

donner du cœur au ventre to put one's heart into it
◖ **regonfler** to boost, pump up again
remonter le moral to boost morale

Gngna.

similar terms

caustique caustic
critique critical
dévalorisant(e) belittling
grossier(-ière) foul-mouthed
insolent(e) cheeky
insultant(e) insulting
ironique ironic
médisant(e) malicious
pince-sans-rire deadpan
sarcastique sarcastic

ironie *f* irony
lazzi *m* scoff, jeer
pique *f* cutting remark
plaisanterie *f* joke
quolibet *m* quip, jibe
ricanement *m* grin, snigger
sarcasme *m* sarcasm

common expressions

◑ **chambrer** to tease
◑ **charrier** to harass
démolir to tear to pieces
être le dindon de la farce to be the laughingstock
◑ **faire un carton sur** to make someone a target
◑ **lancer des vannes** to make wisecracks
mettre en boîte to give someone a hard time, tease
ridiculiser to make fun of
se payer la tête de to make fun of
tourner en ridicule to make fun of, mock

◑ **astuce** *f* **vaseuse** smart-ass remark
blague *f* joke
canular *m* hoax
caricature *f* caricature
dérision *f* derision, ridicule
gag *m* gag, joke
sortie *f* wisecrack, cutting remark
tête *f* **de Turc** whipping boy
◑ **vacherie** *f* cutting remark
◑ **vanne** *f* wisecrack, dig

Encore!

similar terms

amoureux(-euse) in love
engagé(e) committed
enthousiaste enthusiastic
exalté(e) elated
fanatique fanatical, enthusiastic
féru(e) wild (about)
inconditionnel(le) unconditional
sectaire sectarian

adepte *m/f* enthusiast
aficionado *m* devotee
emballement *m* enthusiasm
exaltation *f* elation
fanatisme *m* fanaticism
frénésie *f* frenzy
fureur *f* fury
la passion des livres passion for books
rage *f* rage

avec flamme passionately

avoir le feu sacré to be full of enthusiasm

common expressions

◑ **Je n'en décolle pas!**   I'm hooked!
◑ **Je suis scotché(e)!**   I'm hooked!
◑ **Je suis un(e) allumé(e)!**   I'm a fanatic!

◑ **accro** hooked

un(e) disciple a disciple
un(e) fana a fan
◑ **un(e) pur(e) et dur(e)** a hardliner
◑ **un(e) vrai(e) mordu(e)** a real junkie/fan

similar terms

blasé(e) jaded
dédaigneux(-euse) scornful
froid(e) cold
impassible impassive
imperturbable even-tempered
insensible insensitive

cœur *m* **de pierre** heart of stone
désinvolture *f* offhand manner
détachement *m* detachment
insouciance *f* lack of concern
sécheresse *f* **de cœur** coldhearted attitude

common expressions

Ça me laisse froid(e) / de marbre / de glace.	That leaves me cold.
Je m'en fiche.	I couldn't care less.
Je m'en soucie comme de l'an 40.	Big deal.
Je m'en tape.	I don't give a damn.
Je n'en ai rien à cirer / à foutre / à branler!	I don't give a rat's ass!
Pas mon problème.	Not my problem.
Tu peux crever.	You can go to hell.

Ouf!

similar terms

décharge *f* release
délivrance *f* deliverance
détente *f* relaxation
relâchement *m* relaxation, loosening (up)
alléger to lighten
débarrasser to release (from)
libérer d'un fardeau to relieve of a burden
secourir to rescue

common expressions

C'est pas tombé loin!	Whew! Just missed!
Ça soulage!	What a relief!
Enfin! Sauvé!	Saved at last!
J'en vois le bout!	I see light at the end of the tunnel!
Je l'ai échappée belle!	Lucky me, that was close!
Je m'en suis tiré!	I got out of it!
Je peux souffler!	Now I can breathe!
Je respire!	I can breathe!
Me voilà guéri!	I'm cured!
Ouf! Ça y est!	Whew! That's it, we're there!
Pas trop tôt!	At last!
Un poids en moins!	A weight off my chest!

similar terms

alarme *f* alarm
angoisse *f* **existentielle** existentialist angst
oppression *f* oppression
panique *f* panic
peurs *fpl* fears
phobie *f* phobia
profonde anxiété *f* deep anxiety
tourment *m* torment
vive inquiétude *f* strong concern

common expressions

J'ai peur!	I'm scared!
◑ **Je flippe grave.**	I'm really stressed out.
Je n'ai pas fermé l'œil!	I didn't close my eyes all night!
Je n'arrive pas à me relaxer!	I can't relax!
Je vais craquer!	I'm gonna crack!

céder à la panique to give way to panic
se faire de la bile to fret
se faire des cheveux blancs to worry oneself to death
se faire du mauvais sang to worry

gros soucis *m* huge worry
◑ **mega-stress** *m* enormous amount of stress
◑ **parano** *f* paranoia; *m/f* paranoid person
◑ **prise** *f* **de tête** fit, hassle

What's your mood? Depending on your answer to each of the following questions, you earn one or two points. Answer the questions and add up your score. If you need help, follow the cross-reference to the page(s) indicated.

1 • Vous avez perdu votre cartable avec vos devoirs—il va falloir s'expliquer avec le prof devant toute la classe... Vous flippez grave? Oui (1) ou non (2)? ☞ 77

2 • Votre tante est élue Miss Univers. Vous en restez comme deux ronds de flan? Oui (1) ou non (2)? ☞ 114

3 • À l'arrivée de nouveaux voisins, vous montrez-vous rébarbatif(-ive) (1) ou accueillant(e) (2)? ☞ 80–81

4 • Vos amis luttent pour sauvegarder l'environnement. Vous leur donnez votre soutien (2) ou vous leur lancez des grosses vannes (1)? ☞ 86–87

5 • On essaye de vous faire changer d'avis, mais vous êtes tenace et vous n'en démordrez pas... Oui (2) ou non (1)? ☞ 99

6 • En fin de journée au bureau ou à l'école, êtes-vous complètement lessivé(e)? Oui (1) ou non (2)? ☞ 75

7 • Vous racontez une histoire drôle: généralement vous vous fendez la poire avant la fin? Oui (2) ou non (1)? ☞ 110

8 • Regardez-vous dans la glace. Vous avez la super pêche aujourd'hui? Oui (2) ou non (1)? ☞ 104

9 • Quelqu'un essaye de vous piquer votre iPod. Ça vous fout un peu les boules (2) ou vous pétez carrément les plombs (1)? ☞ 96

10 • En général vous savez prendre du bon temps? Oui (2) ou non (1)? ☞ 95

11 • La semaine commence! Vous en avez marre de cette vie de chien (1) ou vous pétez le feu (2)? ☞ 84–85

12 • Quelqu'un vous rapporte la valise que vous aviez égarée. Vous êtes éperdument reconnaissant(e) qu'on vous ait sorti de la mouise? Oui (2) ou non (1)? ☞ 105

13 • Un chien hurle dans la nuit... Ça vous donne la chair de poule... Oui (1) ou non (2)? ☞ 103

14 • Vous avez une telle imagination que le patron vous a confié le boulot. Vous séchez pendant des heures (1) ou ça a fait tilt tout de suite (2)? ☞ 107

15 • Quand on vous montre la marche à suivre, êtes-vous plutôt attentif(-ive) (2) ou complètement distrait(e)? (1)? ☞ 74

16 • Quand vous pensez à votre enfance, ça vous fait planer (2) ou ça vous fout le cafard (1)? ☞ 78–79

17 • Pendant un vol Air France, une gamine renverse son jus de fraise sur votre chemise. Vous faites juste les gros yeux (2) ou vous lui passez un savon (1)? ☞ 100

18 • Un de vos voisins s'est acheté une Ferrari. Vous en pâlissez d'envie? Oui (1) ou non (2)? ☞ 108

19 • Dans le train, un bébé commence à pleurer. Vous n'y prêtez pas attention (2) ou vous manifestez votre exaspération... (1)? ☞ 115

20 • Vous jouez au tennis: vous avez déjà perdu le premier set 0–6. Vous déchantez un peu (2) ou vous baissez carrément les bras (1)? ☞ 101

21 • Vous êtes généralement content(e) de vous? Oui (2) ou non (1)? ☞ 111

22 • Vous êtes plutôt du genre enthousiaste (2) ou tout vous laisse de marbre (1)? ☞ 88–89

23 • Vous allez chez le percepteur pour un redressement fiscal. Êtes-vous détendu(e) (2) ou plutôt crispé(e) (1)? ☞ 76–77

To see how you did on the Humeuromètre, turn to page 118.

similar terms

affront *m* slight
gros/vilain mot *m* curse word
grossièreté *f* vulgarity
injure *f* insult
invective *f* invective
offense *f* offense
outrage *m* insult

jurons curse words

- **Merde!** Shit!
- **Nom de Dieu!** Christ almighty!
- **Putain!** Holy shit!
- **Putasserie! / Bordel de merde! / Chierie!** Fucking shit!
- **Saloperie!** Horseshit!

insultes insults

- **Abruti!** Moron!
- **Ahuri!** Halfwit!
- **Branleur!** Lazy bum!
- **Conasse! / Sale conne!** Stupid bitch!
- **Connard!** Asshole!
- **Couillon!** Jerk!
- **Crétin!** Moron!
- **Dégonflé!** Coward!
- **Enculé!** Asshole!
- **Enfoiré!** Dumb-ass!
- **Escroc!** Crook!
- **Frimeur!** Show-off!
- **Fumier!** You shit!
- **Garce!** Bitch!
- **Idiot!** Idiot!
- **Imbécile!** Imbecile!
- **Lèche-pompes!** Ass kisser!
- **Magouilleur!** Cheat!
- **Mauviette!** Wimp!
- **Métèque!** *racist slur, usually directed at a swarthy person*
- **Morue!** Bottom-feeder! (*lit.*, cod)
- **Ordure!** Trash!
- **Paumé!** Misfit!
- **Pauvre type!** Bum!
- **Petit con!** Prick!
- **Pimbêche!** Stuck up!
- **Pot de colle!** Leech!
- **Retardé!** Retard!
- **Sac-à-vin!** Drunkard!
- **Sainte nitouche!** Hypocrite!
- **Tordu!** Nutcase!
- **Traîne-lattes!** Lazy bum!

spoken by women only

- **Dragueur!** Womanizer!
- **Goujat!** Cad!
- **Hypocrite!** Hypocrite!
- **Macho!** Chauvinist pig!
- **Maniaque!** Maniac!
- **Maquereau!** Pimp!
- **Obsédé!** Horny bastard!
- **Pervers!** Pervert!
- **Phallocrate!** Chauvinist pig!
- **Salaud!** Bastard!
- **Vicieux!** Pervert!
- **Voyeur!** Peeping Tom!
- **Voyou!** Thug!

HiHi!

similar terms

distraction *f* amusement
divertissement *m* entertainment
partie *f* **de plaisir** fun time
passe-temps *m* hobby
récréation *f* recess
réjouissances *fpl* revelry

passer un bon moment to have a great time
prendre du bon temps to have a nice time
s'amuser to have fun
se relaxer to relax

common expressions

○ **C'est l'éclate!** What fun!
C'est que du bonheur! It's pure fun/happiness!
Ce sont de bons vivants. They are fun-loving people.
Ce sont des fêtards. They are party animals.
Elle est très sympa cette boum/fête! Great party!
Ils savent s'amuser! They sure know how to have fun!
La soirée est très réussie! Great party/evening!
On rigole bien! We're having a good laugh!
○ **On s'en paye une tranche!** We're having lots of fun!
Super ambiance! Great atmosphere!
Vachement convivial! It's pretty friendly here!

faire la bamboula to have a bash
faire la bringue to go on a binge
faire la fête to party
faire la fiesta to live it up
faire la foire to live it up
faire la nouba to live it up

Râârgn!

similar terms

emportement *m* loss of temper
fureur *f* fury
rage *m* rage

éclater to explode
entrer dans une colère noire to fly into a black rage
être à bout to be at the end of one's rope
exploser to explode
voir rouge to see red

colérique angry, short-tempered
irascible hot-tempered
irritable irritable

common expressions

Ça m'énerve!	That bugs me!
Ça me fout les boules!	That pisses me off!
Ça me gonfle!	That really aggravates me!
Ça va péter!	It's gonna blow!
Je me fâche tout rouge!	I'm hopping mad!
Je pète les plombs.	I'm losing it.
Je sors de mes gonds.	I'm coming unhinged.
Je suis en pétard.	I'm about to explode.
Je suis en rogne.	I'm very upset.
Je suis hors de moi!	I'm beside myself!
La colère est mauvaise conseillère.	Anger makes for bad advice.
La moutarde me monte au nez!	I'm losing my temper! (*lit.*, Mustard is going up my nose!)
Maman est très colère!	Mommy is very angry!

monter sur ses grands chevaux to be very angry (*lit.*, to get on one's high horse)

similar terms

attention *f* **soutenue** rapt attention
contemplation *f* contemplation
introspection *f* introspection
méditation *f* meditation
pensée *f* **profonde** deep thought
prière *f* prayer
réflexion *f* **spirituelle** spiritual reflection
vie *f* **intérieure** inner life

focaliser to focus
juger to judge, consider
méditer to meditate
raisonner to reason
réfléchir intensément to think intently
rêver to dream, daydream
s'abîmer dans la réflexion to sink deeply into reflection
s'interroger to wonder (about)
se creuser la tête to think hard
songer to daydream
spéculer to speculate

conscience *f* conscience
entendement *m* understanding
esprit *m* mind
intelligence *f* intelligence
raison *f* reason

common expressions

○ **Ça cogite grave.** The gears are really turning.
Ça donne à réfléchir. It gives one pause.
Il faut peser le pour et le contre. I need to weigh the pros and cons.
Il y a matière à réflexion. It's food for thought.
J'ai besoin de m'isoler du monde extérieur. I have to block out the rest of the world.
J'ai besoin de me concentrer sur moi-même. I have to focus on myself.

○ **Je me sers de ma tronche.** I'm using my head.
Je recentre mon esprit. I am refocusing my mind.
Moi, je fais travailler ma matière grise! My gray matter is working.
Réfléchissons sérieusement. Let's think seriously.

PFFFF!

similar terms

arrogance *f* arrogance
condescendance *f* condescension
dédain *m* disdain
hauteur *f* aloofness
indifférence *f* indifference
morgue *f* contempt, haughtiness

crâneur(-euse) pretentious; *m/f* show-off
frimeur(-euse) stuck-up; *m/f* show-off
ignoble sordid
méprisable despicable

common expressions

Elle le prend de haut.	She looks down her nose at people.
Elle vous toise du haut de sa grandeur.	She looks you up and down.
Fi!	Pfft!
Ils ne m'arrivent pas à la cheville!	They can't hold a candle to me!
Je les conspue!	Raspberries to them!
Je les emmerde, à pied, à cheval et en voiture!	Screw them! (*lit.*, I shit on them when I'm walking, riding a horse, or driving!)
Je les foule aux pieds.	I walk all over them.
Je les hais.	I hate them.
Je les nargue!	I taunt them!
Je les snobe.	I snub them.
La bave du crapaud n'atteint pas la blanche colombe.	Sticks and stones may break my bones, but words will never hurt me. (*lit.*, The drool of the frog can't reach the white dove.)
Le roi n'est pas son cousin.	He thinks he's the cat's meow. / He doesn't need anybody else. (*lit.*, The king is not his cousin.)

fier (fière) comme Artaban proud as a peacock

similar terms

autodétermination *f* self-determination
décision *f* decision
engagement *m* commitment
entêtement *m* stubbornness
motivation *f* motivation
persistance *f* persistence
résolution *f* resolution

cabochard(e) pig-headed, stubborn
obstiné(e) obstinate
opiniâtre headstrong
tenace tenacious, persistent
têtu(e) stubborn
volontaire willful

tenir bon, jusqu'au bout to hold out till the bitter end

common expressions

C'est une idée fixe.	It's an obsession.
J'y arriverai.	I'll manage.
J'y suis résolu(e) de tout mon être.	I'm determined with all my being.
Je focalise grave.	I'm concentrating hard.
Je le soutiens mordicus.	I'm standing firm.
Je n'en démords pas.	I won't let go of it.
Je ne lâcherai pas prise.	I won't give up.
Je vais le mener à bien.	I'll see it through.

similar terms

blâme *m* blame
condamnation *f* condemnation
désaccord *m* disagreement
mécontentement *m* dissatisfaction
refus *m* refusal
rejet *m* rejection
reproche *m* reproach

faire les gros yeux to glare (at)
froncer les sourcils to frown

œil *m* **réprobateur** disapproving eye

common expressions

Au fait, vous êtes viré!	By the way, you're fired!
C'est contre mes principes!	It's against my principles!
C'est inacceptable!	Unacceptable!
Jamais de la vie!	No way!
Je réprouve!	I don't approve!
◑ Le dirlo va vous passer un sacré savon!	The boss is gonna let you have it!
Où vous croyez-vous?	Where do you think you are?
Pas d'accord!	Not okay! / I disagree!
◑ Pas de ça, Lisette!	No way, José!
Pour qui vous prenez-vous?	Who do you think you are?
Son visage reflète la désapprobation.	Her face shows her disapproval.
Vous allez vous faire remonter les bretelles.	You're gonna catch some flack.

le découragement | discouragement

Bah!

similar terms

accablement *m* dejection
amère/cruelle déception *f* bitter/cruel disappointment
déboires *mpl* disillusionment
défaite *f* defeat
dépit *m* bitter disappointment
désespoir *m* despair
détresse *f* distress
échec *m* failure
fiasco *m* failure
grise mine *f* disappointed look
illusions *fpl* **perdues** lost illusions
lassitude *f* weariness
mauvaise surprise *f* unpleasant surprise
perte *f* **de courage/moral** loss of courage/morale

déçu(e) disappointed
défrisé(e) disappointed

abandonner to give up
baisser les bras to give up
capituler to capitulate

démissionner to quit
se résigner to resign

common expressions

Bah, à quoi bon...?	What's the use ...?
C'est fini, foutu.	It's over, all screwed up.
J'ai craqué.	I broke down.
J'ai la queue entre les jambes.	I'm disappointed. (*lit.*, I've got my tail between my legs.)
J'ai le moral à zéro.	I'm down in the dumps.
J'ai ramassé une veste.	I failed.
J'en suis bien revenu(e)!	Boy, am I glad I'm back!
Je déchante.	I'm disappointed.
Je laisse tomber.	I give up.
Je me suis planté.	I screwed up.
Je ne vois pas le bout du tunnel.	I don't see light at the end of the tunnel.
Je suis gros Jean comme devant.	I got nothing out of it.
Le moral est au plus bas.	Morale is at a low point.
Tout est nul.	Everything is worthless.

être au bout du rouleau to be at the end of one's rope
jeter l'éponge to throw in the towel

largué(e) out of it

un(e) perdant(e) a loser

Heu...

similar terms

embarras *m* embarrassment
honte *f* shame
malaise *f* uneasiness
trouble *m* confusion

emprunté(e) awkward
ennuyé(e) embarrassed
gauche clumsy
guindé(e) stiff, formal

être intimidé(e) to be intimidated

common expressions

◗ Bonjour le malaise!	Boy, am I embarrassed!
C'est la honte!	Boy, how embarrassing!
Je bafouille.	I'm babbling.
◗ Je grimpe dans le cerisier!	I'm red in the face with shame (*lit.*, up in the cherry tree)!
Je me fais tout(e) petit(e).	I'm making myself very tiny.
◗ Je me sens godiche et cucu!	I feel silly and dumb!
Je ne sais plus où me mettre.	I don't know where to hide.
Je rougis/pique un fard!	I'm turning red as a beet!

être mal à l'aise to be ill at ease
être rose de confusion to blush with embarrassment
être rouge de honte to blush with shame
ne pas savoir sur quel pied danser to not know which foot to lead with
rire jaune to laugh nervously

AAAAH!

similar terms

affolement *m* panic
alarme *f* alarm
la chair de poule goosebumps
crainte *f* dread
effroi *m* terror
épouvante *f* fright, horror
des frissons *mpl* shivers
panique *f* panic
terreur *f* terror

craintif(-ive) fearful
inquiet(e) anxious
lâche chicken, yellow; *m/f* coward
poltron(ne) cowardly; *m/f* coward

avoir des sueurs froides to break out in a cold sweat
sursauter to jump, start

common expressions

À vous glacer le sang!	It makes your blood run cold!
◑ Ça fout la trouille / la pétoche / les jetons!	That gives me the willies/jitters/creeps!
J'ai eu une peur bleue.	I had a bad scare.
◑ J'ai les grelots!	I'm shivering!
J'en tremble encore!	I'm still shaking!
Je claque des dents!	My teeth are chattering!
◑ Je fais dans mon froc!	I'm shitting my pants!
◑ Je serre les fesses.	I'm scared stiff.
◑ Je suis mort(e) de trouille.	I'm scared to death.

◑ **dégonflé(e)** deflated; *m/f* chicken, coward
◑ **pétochard(e)** cowardly; *m/f* chicken
◑ **trouillard(e)** lily-livered; *m/f* chicken

◑ **la grosse frayeur** the ultimate scare
◑ **mouille-cul** *m* pants-wetter, chicken
◑ **un trac monstre** big-time stage fright

good shape | en forme

Hop!

similar terms

avoir la santé to be in good health
être dans une excellente forme physique
   to be in great shape
être en train to be full of energy

beau comme Apollon handsome as Apollo
frais comme un gardon fresh as a daisy
frais et dispos bright eyed and bushy tailed
Elle a une jolie silhouette. She has a nice
   figure.
Elle a une taille de guêpe. She has a narrow
   waist.

common expressions

Ç'est le manque d'exercice.   It's due to lack of exercise.
◑ Depuis que j'ai arrêté de fumer,   Since I quit smoking, I'm full of
   je pète le feu!   energy!
Faut que je me refasse un ventre.   I've got to rebuild my abs.
◑ J'ai bouffé du lion!   I'm full of energy!
◑ J'ai un peu de bide.   I've got a bit of a paunch.
◑ J'ai une frite!   I'm in incredible shape!
◑ J'ai une pêche!   I'm in terrific shape!
◑ Je bouffe trop.   I eat too much.
Je me mets au régime!   I'm going on a diet!
◑ Je suis regonflé(e) à bloc!   I'm back in top form!
Je tiens une forme olympique!   I'm in Olympic form!

faire de la gym to go to the gym
faire de la muscu to work out
faire du sport to play sports

104   **moods, emotions, and attitudes**

Merci!

similar terms

gratitude *f* gratitude, thanks

être éperdu(e) de reconnaissance to be deeply grateful

être éternellement reconnaissant(e)/redevable to be eternally grateful

être obligé(e) to be indebted

être redevable to be indebted

payer de retour to pay back

savoir gré to be grateful

common expressions

Il n'a même pas la reconnaissance du ventre.	He forgets what we did for him.
Je suis votre débiteur.	I'm in your debt.
Je vous dois une fière chandelle / la vie.	I owe you big time / my life.
Mille grâces.	A thousand thanks.
Vous m'avez sorti de la merde / du pétrin / de la mouise.	You pulled me out of the shit / my misery.
Vous me retirez une sacrée épine du pied.	You saved my life. (*lit.*, You pulled a splinter from my foot.)
Vous n'obligerez pas un(e) ingrat(e).	I won't be ungrateful. (*lit.*, You didn't help an ingrate.)

Grmmb...

similar terms

dissimulation *f* deception
duplicité *f* duplicity
fourberie *f* deceit
mensonge *m* **par omission** lie by omission

ambigu(ë) ambiguous
déloyal(e) disloyal
faux (fausse) fake
flatteur(-euse) flattering, sycophantic; *m/f* sycophant
furtif(-ive) furtive
menteur(-euse) lying; *m/f* liar
mielleux(-euse) fawning
perfide perfidious; *m/f* traitor
sournois(e) sly
traître(sse) treacherous; *m/f* traitor

agir de biais / par en dessous to act in a roundabout fashion / behind someone's back
agir en douce / par-derrière / sous le manteau to act incognito / behind someone's back / in disguise
faire l'hypocrite to be a hypocrite
faire l'innocent to play the innocent
retourner sa veste to change sides

common expressions

Il est faux-cul! — He's a two-faced bastard!
On lui donnerait le Bon Dieu sans confession. — He looks as if butter wouldn't melt in his mouth. (*lit.,* You'd give him communion without confession.)

Son petit air d'en avoir deux. — He's got the look of a double-dealer.
Tout sucre et tout miel. — All sugar and honey.

manger à tous les râteliers to do what's most convenient
noyer le poisson to try to talk one's way out

coup *m* **de Jarnac** stab in the back
double jeu *m* double game
faux-jeton *m* hypocrite
Judas *m* Judas
lèche-cul *m* brownnoser, ass kisser
petit saint *m/f* saint-pretender
sainte nitouche *f* Goody Two-shoes
Scapin *m* double-crosser (character in a Molière play)
Tartuffe *m* traitor (character in a Molière play)

Eurêka!

similar terms

association *f* **d'idées** association of ideas
concept *m* concept
conscience *f* awareness
courant *m* **de pensée** intellectual trend
découverte *f* discovery
humour *m* humor
imagination *f* imagination
invention *f* invention
notion *f* notion
trouvaille *f* flash

créatif(-ive) creative
intelligent(e) intelligent
malin (maligne) clever
pétillant(e) bubbly

avoir une idée to have an idea
trouver la solution to find the solution

common expressions

Aucune idée!	I don't have a clue!
Ça a fait tilt!	The idea popped up out of nowhere!
Ça carbure, ça cogite!	The motor's running, something's stirring!
Ça vous donne une idée / un aperçu du cerveau humain.	This gives you a hint about / an insight into the human brain.
J'ai ma petite idée là-dessus.	I have an idea about this.
Je ne cherche pas, je trouve. (Picasso)	I don't seek, I find.
On ne m'ôtera pas de l'idée que...	I'm still convinced that ...
Riche idée que j'ai eue là!	A bright idea I had there!

avoir plein d'idées to have plenty of ideas
être à court d'idées to be short of ideas
plancher to cram (study)
se creuser to rack one's brains
sécher to come up empty

MMhh...

similar terms

aigreur *f* bitterness
concurrence *f* competition
dépit *m* disappointment
désir *m* desire, envy
envie *f* envy
haine *f* hatred
plagiat *m* plagiarism

méfiance *f* distrust
rivalité *f* rivalry
soupçon *m* suspicion
surveillance *f* surveillance

convoiter to covet
jalouser to be jealous of
pâlir d'envie to be green with envy

en baver drooling (over)
en crever consumed with jealousy
envieux(-euse) du bien d'autrui envious of people's property

common expressions

Ça m'a mis la puce à l'oreille!	That set me to thinking.
Chat échaudé craint l'eau froide.	Once bitten, twice shy.
◑ Faire gaffe!	Better watch out!
Il y a anguille sous roche.	There's something going on.
	(*lit.*, There's an eel under the rock.)
◑ Il y a un truc qui cloche.	Something's not right.
◑ Je flaire le lézard.	I smell a rat.
Je reste sur le qui-vive.	I'm on the alert.
◑ On ne me la fait pas!	You can't con me!
Ouvrons l'œil!	Keep your eyes open!
◑ Toi mon gaillard, je t'ai à l'œil.	Dude, I've got my eye on you.

être soupçonneux(-euse) to be suspicious
◑ **être un brin parano** to be feeling paranoid
se douter de quelque chose to suspect something
se méfier to beware, distrust
se tenir sur ses gardes to be on one's guard
subodorer/deviner/flairer to smell a rat

jaloux(-ouse) comme un tigre extremely jealous
malade de jalousie sick with jealousy

Yahou!

similar terms

bonheur *m* **ineffable** unbelievable happiness
délire *m* delirium
euphorie *f* euphoria
explosion *f* **de joie** outburst of joy
exultation *f* exultation
une joie indicible indescribable joy
liesse *f* bliss

common expressions

C'est l'éclate!	It's a blast!
C'est le pied!	That's terrific!
Je m'en donne à cœur joie!	I'm elated!
Je n'ai jamais été à pareille fête!	I've never had such a feast!
Je nage dans le bonheur!	I'm basking in happiness!
Je ne vous raconte pas: c'est que du bonheur!	I can't describe it—it's pure happiness!
Je plane!	I'm floating on air!
Je suis aux anges / au 7ème ciel!	I'm on cloud nine / in seventh heaven!
Youpi!	Yippee! Yahoo!

HAHA!

similar terms

fou-rire *m* **nerveux** nervous laugh
hilarité *f* hilarity
rigolade *f* laughter

glousser to chuckle
plaisanter to joke
pouffer to burst out laughing
rigoler to laugh
s'esclaffer to guffaw

common expressions

À mourir de rire!	You'll die laughing!
Arrête, je suis plié!	Stop, I'm doubled over with laughter!
C'est d'un drôle!	It's too funny!
◑ C'est poilant / hilarant / à hurler.	It's hilarious.
◑ On se fend la pipe/poire/pêche/ gueule.	I split a gut laughing.
◑ On se pisse dessus de rire!	I'm laughing so hard, I'm peeing!

éclater de rire to burst out laughing
rire à gorge déployée to roar with laughter
rire aux larmes to laugh till one cries
rire jaune to laugh nervously
rire sous cape / dans sa barbe to laugh up one's sleeve
◑ **se marrer comme une baleine / un bossu / un dératé /
   un fou (une folle)** to laugh like a whale/hunchback/nut/fool
se plier to double over with laughter
se rire du danger to laugh at danger
se taper sur les cuisses to slap your thighs (from laughing)
se tenir les côtes to split one's sides (from laughing)
se tordre de rire to double over with laughter

similar terms

bonheur *m* happiness
contentement *m* contentment, satisfaction
plaisir *m* pleasure
sérénité *f* serenity

béat(e) joyful
bien aise glad, very pleased
comblé(e) filled with contentment
ravi(e) thrilled
serein(e) serene

common expressions

C'est parfait!	It's perfect!
Je me sens bien!	I feel good!
Je suis comblé(e)!	I'm thrilled!
Je suis content(e) de moi!	I'm proud of myself!
Mission accomplie.	Mission accomplished.
Satisfaction du devoir accompli.	The satisfaction of a job well done.

en accord/harmonie avec soi-même in harmony with one's self
en paix at peace

similar terms

assoupissement *m* drowsiness
endormissement *m* falling asleep
insomnie *f* insomnia
repos *m* rest
somme *m* sleep, nap
sommeil *f* sleep
somnolence *f* drowsiness
trouble *m* **du sommeil** trouble sleeping

à poings fermés fast asleep
endormi(e) asleep
veille awake

common expressions

J'ai passé une nuit blanche.	I was up all night.
Je n'ai pas fermé l'œil.	I didn't close my eyes all night.
Je suis insomniaque.	I'm an insomniac.

avoir de la difficulté à s'endormir to have trouble sleeping
compter les moutons to count sheep
dormir debout to fall asleep on one's feet
dormir du sommeil du juste to sleep the sleep of the just
en écraser to sleep soundly
faire une petite sieste to take a nap
pioncer to sleep
➲ **piquer un roupillon** to catch a nap
➲ **piquer une ronflette** to have a snooze
ronfler comme une bête to sleep (*lit.*, snore) like a pig

dans les bras de Morphée in the arms of Morpheus (the god of dreams)

couche-tard *m/f* night owl
cure *f* **de sommeil** sleep therapy
lève-tard *m/f* late riser
lève-tôt *m/f* early riser
oiseau *m* **de nuit** night owl
réveils *mpl* **intempestifs** troubled sleep
un sommeil de plomb a heavy sleep
un sommeil léger a light sleep
un sommeil réparateur a refreshing sleep

Aïe!

similar terms

douleur *f* pain
une douleur atroce/sourde/pressante
  an awful pain
peine *f* sorrow
tourment *m* torment

compatir à la douleur de quelqu'un
  to feel for someone in his/her sorrow
endurer/subir/vivre un véritable calvaire
  to go through a real ordeal
se tordre de douleur to writhe in pain
souffrir le martyre to suffer agony
traverser une terrible épreuve physique
  to go through a tremendous physical ordeal

common expressions

Aïaïaïe! Je souffre dans ma chair!	Oh my God! It hurts!
Bobo!	Ouch!
C'est à hurler!	It makes me scream!
C'est hyper douloureux!	It hurts like hell!
C'est intolérable!	I can't take it!
Ça fait très très mal!	It really hurts!
J'en ai bavé.	I had a hard time.
⟡ J'en chie!	I've got a hell of a pain!
⟡ Je le sens passer!	The pain's going right through me!
⟡ La vache, je morfle un max!	Holy cow, I put up with a lot!
Les grandes douleurs sont muettes.	The greatest suffering is done in silence.
Ouille!	Ouch!

Quoi! Non?

similar terms

déni *m* denial
doute *f* doubt
étonnement *m* astonishment
hébétude *f* stupefaction
incrédulité *f* disbelief
perplexité *f* bewilderment
stupeur *f* amazement

abasourdi(e) aghast
interloqué(e) awestruck

être sceptique to be skeptical
exiger des preuves to require proof
nier to deny
rester pantois(e) to be dumbfounded
tomber des nues to be flabbergasted

common expressions

C'est une plaisanterie!	It's a joke!
Ça alors, pour une surprise!	Boy, what a surprise!
Dites-moi que je rêve!	Tell me I'm dreaming!
J'en suis resté comme deux ronds de flan!	I was stunned!
Je n'en crois pas mes oreilles/yeux!	I don't believe my ears/eyes!
Je n'en reviens pas!	I can't get over it!
Je suis comme St Thomas.	I'm doubtful (*lit.*, like St. Thomas).
◗ Je suis sur les fesses / sous le choc!	I've been thrown for a loop! I'm in shock!
◗ Je tombe de haut!	I'm flabbergasted.
Les bras m'en tombent!	I'm astounded!
◗ On se fout de ma gueule!?	They think I'm an idiot!?

similar terms

exaspération *f* exasperation
irritabilité *f* irritability
mécontentement *m* dissatisfaction
sensibilité *f* sensitivity
une sensibilité à fleur de peau
  a hypersensitivity

chatouilleux(-euse) sensitive, ticklish
délicat(e) delicate, sensitive
irascible touchy
ombrageux(-euse) skittish
pointilleux(-euse) fussy
sensible sensitive

common expressions

C'est un(e) écorché(e) vif (vive).	He's/She's got thin skin.
C'est un(e) épidermique.	He/She can't take it.
C'est un(e) hyper sensible.	He's/She's highly sensitive.
○ Elle est méga parano!	She's a big-time paranoid!
○ Il faut surtout pas l'emmerder.	Don't bug her.
Il part au quart de tour.	He's angry right from the start.
Il prend la mouche pour un rien.	He's easily upset.
Il prend tout de travers.	He takes everything the wrong way.
Tout de suite les mots qui blessent.	Nasty words right off the bat.

similar terms

dilemme *m* dilemma
doute *f* doubt
hésitation *f* hesitation
indécision *f* indecision
inquiétude *f* worry
insécurité *f* insecurity
perplexité *f* puzzlement, confusion
le principe d'Heisenberg Heisenberg's
   uncertainty principle

flou(e) blurry
hésitant(e) hesitating
indécis(e) indecisive
indéterminé(e) uncertain
vague vague

common expressions

À quel saint se vouer?	Which way to turn? (*lit.*, Which saint should we pray to?)
◑ Ça ballotte grave.	We don't know who won yet. (The ballots are being counted, and the election is very close.)
Dans le doute, abstiens-toi.	When in doubt, do nothing.
L'avenir est incertain.	The future is uncertain.
On avance à tâtons / dans le brouillard / à l'aveuglette…	We're feeling our way in the dark …
◑ On est complètement paumés.	We're completely lost.
On n'est plus sûr de rien.	We're not sure of anything.
On se perd en conjectures.	We're just making things up.
On tergiverse.	We're waffling.

OOOOH!

similar terms

admiration *f* admiration
éblouissement *m* amazement
enchantement *m* enchantment
enthousiasme *f* enthusiasm
ravissement *m* rapture

abasourdi(e) amazed
ébloui(e) par le spectacle dazzled by the show
fasciné(e) fascinated
stupéfait(e) astounded

être ébahi to be dumbfounded

common expressions

C'est magique!	It's magic!
C'est rien que du bonheur!	It's pure happiness!
C'est sublime!	It's wonderful!
Grandiose!	Spectacular!
J'ai les yeux comme des soucoupes!	My eyes are as big as saucers!
J'en ai plein les mirettes!	I'm dazzled!
J'en bave des ronds de chapeau!	How incredibly surprising!
J'en suis bouche bée!	My mouth is wide open!
J'en tombe sur les fesses!	It knocked me over!
Quelle beauté!	What a beauty!
Superbe!	Superb!

Let's see how you did on the Humeuromètre (pages 92–93) and what it reveals about your mood!

23–30 Ouh là là! Dites donc, ce n'est pas la joie aujourd'hui! Pour un rien vous montez sur vos grands chevaux ou vous descendez au 36ème dessous! Faites un petit sourire à votre entourage, ça leur fera des vacances!

31–38 Vous êtes d'humeur plutôt égale. Même contrarié(e) vous affrontez les choses avec philosophie. Vous ne prenez pas trop la grosse tête. On aurait besoin de plus de gens comme vous dans l'administration française!

39–46 Votre côté résolument optimiste et positif fait plaisir à voir, bien qu'il puisse s'avérer légèrement oppressant pour les gens qui nagent dans les problèmes à longueur de journée. Mais comme vous leur apportez aussi des solutions, ils n'ont pas trop à se plaindre.

appearance and gestures

afro
Afro

banane du rocker
rocker, Elvis cut

bouclés
curly

crêpés/choucroute
bouffant, updo, beehive

**boule à zéro
(style légion)**
*shaved head
(Marine style)*

chignon
bun

related expressions

la chevelure hair
cuir chevelu *m* scalp
mèche *f* **de cheveux** lock, strand
◑ **les plumes** *fpl* hair
racine *f* root
◑ **les tifs** *mpl* hair
touffe *f* tuft

• • •

genre *m* **de cheveux** type of hair

les cheveux *mpl* ____ ____ hair
  bouclés curly
  brillants shiny
  courts short
  crépus frizzy
  en brosse flattop
  fins fine

frisés curly
gominés slicked-back/gelled
gras greasy
laqués shiny
longs long
ondulés wavy
plaqués cornrow
plats straight
qui cassent brittle
raides stiff
séborrhée oily
secs dry
souples soft
soyeux silky
ternes dull

• • •

couettes
pigtails

coupe au bol
bowl cut, dutch boy

courts
short

en arrière
*off the face,
pulled/combed back*

crépus
frizzy

en brosse
flattop

couleur *f* **des cheveux** hair color
les cheveux _____ _____ hair
  aile de corbeau raven black
  argentés silvery
  auburn auburn
  blonds (strawberry-)blonde
  bruns brown
  châtains light brown
  d'ébène jet black
  gris gray
  grisonnants graying
  noirs black
  poivre et sel salt-and-pepper
  roux reddish
le premier cheveu blanc the first
  white hair

«Respecte mes cheveux blancs
  et mon grand âge, petit
  morveux!» "Have respect for
  my white hair and my age,
  you little snot nose!"

• • •

volume *m* **de cheveux** hair
  thickness
les cheveux _____ _____ hair
  abondants lots of
  clairsemés thin
  drus thick
  épais thick, lush
  fins fine
  rares thin

frange devant
bangs

gominés
slicked back / gelled

hippie (à la Jésus)
hippie

**nuque longue
(coupe Longueuil)**
mullet

punk (iroquois)
punk, mohawk

palmier
coconut

calvitie *f* baldness
chauve *m/f* chrome dome; *adj* bald
crinière *f* mane, mop
implant *m* **de cheveux**
  hair transplant
toison *f* mane

perdre ses cheveux to lose one's
  hair
se déplumer to lose one's hair,
  go bald

• • •

les cheveux en désordre
  hair in a mess
les cheveux _____ _____ hair
  dépeignés ruffled
  ébouriffés tousled
  échevelés tousled

emmêlés tangled
en bataille tousled
en broussaille tousled
en coup de vent windblown
en pétard windblown
hirsutes unkempt

épi *m* tuft of hair
frange *f* bangs
houppe/houppette *f* tuft of hair
mèche *f* lock, strand
nattes *fpl* braids
queue *f* **de cheval** ponytail
raie *f* **au milieu** part in the middle
raie *f* **sur le côté** part on the side

brosser to brush
démêler to untangle
être décoiffé(e) to have messy hair
peigner to comb

queue de cheval
ponytail

queue de rat
rattail

raie au milieu
parted in the middle

rasé
shaved

raie sur le côté
parted on the side

rastaquouère
(style Jamaïque)
dreadlocks, braids
(Jamaican style)

● ● ●

accessoires *mpl* accessories
barrette *f* barrette
épingle *f* pin
filet *m* hairnet
nœud *f* bow
peigne *m* comb
pince *f* **à cheveux** hair clip/clasp
résille *f* hairnet
ruban *m* ribbon
serre-tête *m* headband

cheveu *m* **d'ange** angel hair
faux cheveux *mpl* fake hair
moumoute *f* toupee
perruque *f* wig
postiche *m* hairpiece, toupee, wig
rajouts *mpl* hair extensions
toupet *m* toupee

● ● ●

soins *mpl* **des cheveux** hair care
bigoudi *m* hair curler/roller
brillantine *f* hair cream
brossage *m* brushing
brushing *m* blow-dry
coiffure *f* hairdo, hairstyle
coloration *f* hair dyeing/tinting
une coupe de cheveux a haircut
des poux *mpl* lice
fer *m* **à friser** curling iron
gel *m* gel
indéfrisable *f* perm(anent)
laque *f* hairspray
mousse *f* **coiffante** hair mousse
permanente *f* perm(anent)
pommade *f* pomade
rouleau *m* hair curler/roller

tresses plaquées
cornrows

tresses/nattes
braids

salon *m* **de coiffure** hair salon/ stylist
sèche-cheveux *m* hair dryer
shampooing *m* shampoo
teinture *f* dye
aller chez le coiffeur to go to the barber shop/hairdresser's
arranger ses cheveux to fix one's hair
avoir des parasites to get head lice
couper to cut
désépaissir to thin (out), trim
effiler to trim
faire une mise en plis to set someone's hair, perm

lustrer to make shine
rafraîchir to neaten up
se coiffer to comb/brush one's hair
se décolorer to bleach
se faire un shampooing to shampoo one's hair
se laver les cheveux to wash one's hair
se teindre to dye
tailler to trim
tondre to shave off, shear
chez le coiffeur to the hairdresser
chez le coupe-tifs to/at the hair salon/stylist

• • •

À un cheveu près.
That's close.
Fin comme un cheveu.
Within a hair's breadth.
Il s'en est fallu d'un cheveu.
That was close.
Il y a un cheveu.
There's a snag/hitch.
Ne pas toucher à un cheveu de quelqu'un. Don't touch a hair on someone's head.
T'es un coupeur de cheveux en quatre! You're splitting hairs!
Tu arrives comme un cheveu sur la soupe! You come at a bad time!

avoir mal aux cheveux / avoir la gueule de bois to have a hangover
avoir un cheveu sur la langue to lisp
être tiré par les cheveux to be far-fetched
faire dresser les cheveux sur la tête to make someone's hair stand on end
s'arracher les cheveux to tear one's hair out (with worry)
se crêper le chignon to scratch each other's eyes out
se faire des cheveux (blancs) to worry oneself to death

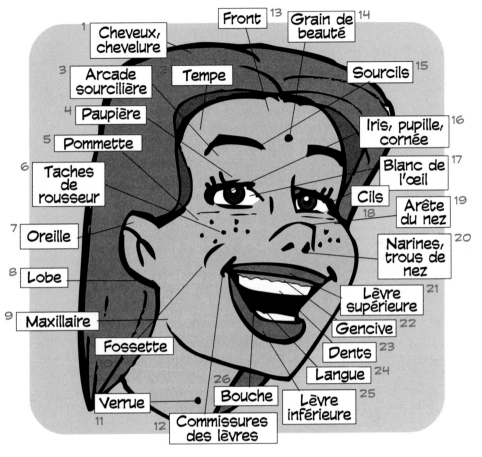

1 · Hair
2 · Temple
3 · Arch of the eyebrow
4 · Eyelid
5 · Cheek
6 · Freckles
7 · Ear
8 · Earlobe
9 · Jawbone
10 · Dimple
11 · Wart
12 · Corners of the mouth

13 · Forehead
14 · Beauty spot
15 · Eyebrows
16 · Iris, pupil, cornea
17 · White of the eye
18 · Eyelashes
19 · Tip of the nose
20 · Nostrils
21 · Upper lip
22 · Gums
23 · Teeth
24 · Tongue
25 · Lower lip
26 · Mouth

**anguleux,
taillé à la serpe**
angular, craggy

**allongé,
en lame de couteau**
elongated, hatchet face

**aux pommettes
saillantes**
with high cheekbones

**bouffi, ravagé,
chiffonné**
*swollen, ravaged,
tired-looking*

**fin,
aux traits réguliers**
*with fine features,
with harmonious features*

chevalin
horsy

**mafflu, empâté,
adipeux, gros**
thick, puffy, fat, fleshy

**irrégulier,
asymétrique**
irregular, crooked

**osseux, maigre,
émacié**
bony, thin, emaciated

ovale
oval

poupin, joufflu
chubby

prognathe, menton proéminent / en galoche
with a prominent chin

related expressions

couleur *f* **naturelle du visage**
  natural color
grain *m* **de la peau**
  skin complexion
minois *m* fresh young face
rides *fpl* wrinkles
teint *m* skin tone

agréable good-looking
frimousse bright-faced

**analyse du caractère d'après la
  forme du visage (physionomie)**
  judging a person on facial
  appearance (physiognomy)
faciès *m* face, bearing
figure *f* figure
lignes *fpl* **du visage** facial structure
masque *f* mask
tête *f* head
traits *mpl* features

•••

le visage _____ _____ face
  basané sunburned
  blafard pale
  blême pale, ashen
  boutonneux pimply
  bronzé tanned
  couperosé blotchy
  crispé shriveled
  fané faded
  flétri dried-up
  grêlé pock-marked
  pâle pale
  ravagé ravaged
  ridé wrinkled
  tanné tanned
  terreux ashen

•••

**rond,
en pleine lune**
round

**ridé, plissé,
parcheminé**
wrinkled, lined, rutted

simiesque
ape-like

le visage ____ ____ face
  décomposé distraught
  défait haggard
  détendu relaxed
  énergique energetic
  fatigué tired
  hermétique poker
  maussade sullen
  mignon cute
  rayonnant radiant
  renfrogné frowning, sullen
  reposé rested
  sérieux serious
  sévère stern
  souriant smiling
  tourmenté contorted
  tranquille calm

•••

lifting *m* face-lift
maquillage *m* makeup
rajeunissement *m* **du visage**
  facial rejuvenation
soins *mpl* **de beauté** beauty care
soins *mpl* **du visage** facial

avoir bonne mine to look good

avoir bonne mine to look good

Elle respire la santé et la joie de vivre. Ses joues roses, elle les doit à son séjour à la mer! En fait, elle est en pleine forme. Elle a le visage frais, coloré, radieux! She looks healthy and fit. Her cheeks are pink as roses, thanks to a trip to the beach! She's in terrific shape. Her face is fresh, full of color, and beaming!

avoir mauvaise mine to look lousy

Ce type a le masque. Il a les traits tirés, la mine défaite. Il a une gueule de lendemain de bringue (avec gueule de bois). Il broie du noir. (Il a le cafard, le bourdon. Pas le moral du tout.) Il est blême, très pâlichon. Teint blafard, mine de papier mâché. He looks like death warmed over. His features are stretched, and he looks beat. He looks like he's got a hangover. He's down in the dumps! He's pale and peaked. His skin is sallow, and he has a ghostly appearance.

Il a une des ces formes! Il a la frite! La pêche! He's in terrific shape!

Il pète de santé. Ce mec a l'air rayonnant, heureux, éveillé, ouvert, avenant. He glows with good health. This guy beams; he looks happy, alert, open, and attractive.

collet monté uptight

Elle a cet air engoncé de ceux qui ont avalé un cintre. Cette dame a la bouche en cul de poule. Elle est du genre coincé. She looks like she's got a poker up her rear (*lit.*, swallowed a hanger). Her mouth is as tight as a chicken's butt hole. She's pretty uptight.

placide easygoing

Lorsqu'on est, comme Charles, débonnaire, placide, tolérant et philosophe, on prend la vie du bon côté! On a les traits reposés. People like Charles are good-natured, calm, open-minded, and philosophical. They take life as it comes. They look rested and relaxed.

poches sous les yeux bags under the eyes

Celui-ci, malgré sa petite mine, va bien. Mais il a des valises sous les yeux tellement énormes qu'il a toujours des problèmes pour passer la douane. This guy, in spite of his feeble appearance, is actually fine. But he has such big bags under his eyes that he has to pay a surcharge when he flies.

Meanwhile, down at the police station, the sketch artist is confronted by discrepancies in the witnesses' descriptions of a pickpocket. Read what the witnesses report, then turn the page to view his identi-kit sketches of the person the police are looking for.

COP *It's a "facemaking" session! Our artist from the Anthropometry and Physiognomy Department needs your testimony to draw a portrait of the pickpocket.*

WITNESS 1 *The man had a masculine face, with strong bone structure, a rounded forehead and receding hairline, a piercing look from deep-set eyes and thick, bushy eyebrows, a smashed-in nose, and a square jaw. With a wrinkle across his forehead, he looked like he was stressed out.*

WITNESS 2 *He had a sneaky air about him, a weird face, a fishy look ... I remember a big Adam's apple topped by a thug's face, with a harelip and bad teeth!*

WITNESS 3 *This bearded dude had an ordinary look, a plain face, vacant and dull eyes, with no expression, droopy eyelids, and bags under his eyes, a bent nose and chapped lips, all cracked. Here's the key: He took my watch!*

WITNESS 4 *A high forehead that juts out, slanty, sleepy, almond-shaped eyes with dilated pupils, cauliflower ears, dilated nostrils, a hooked nose, a scar on his temple, hollow cheeks, canine teeth, and a weak chin. If it helps, he looks like my inbred cousin.*

WITNESS 5 *Rather handsome, stylish, and elegant, with a nose like a trumpet, gap teeth, two smile lines, delicately shaped ears, and, above all, thick, sensuous, sexy lips. His open, radiant face made a strong impression ... I saw a malicious gleam in his amused look and crow's-feet at the corners of his eyes, when I trusted him with my purse.*

WITNESS 6 *I'm still shaking from his dark, shifty look; his eyes were sinister, bulging almost out of their sockets, with rings under them and big bags, toothless, a scar on one of his jowls, his turkey neck with flabby, saggy skin, and pale, translucent skin with the veins clearly visible ...*

WITNESS 7 *He had huge bags under his eyes ... but maybe that's normal for a pickpocket ...*

related terms

air/aspect *m* look
allure *f* bearing
apparence *f* appearance
aspect *m* extérieur outward
  appearance
attitude *f* attitude
caractère *m* character
contenance *f* bearing
coupe *f* / dégaine *f* / tournure *f*
  look
les dehors *mpl* overall look
effigie *f* effigy, image
ensemble *m* / tenue *f* outfit

image *f* image
mimique *f* facial expression
mine *f* look (face, body, or health)
personnage *m* character
personnalité *f* personality
physionomie *f* physiognomy
port *f* de tête carriage of one's head
présentation *f* presentation
profil *m* profile
silhouette *f* silhouette
stature *f* stature
style *m* style

Flic Séance de trombinoscope! Notre artiste du département Anthropométrie et Physiognomonie attend vos témoignages pour réaliser un portrait robot du voleur à la tire.

1 L'homme avait une figure virile, à l'ossature forte, un front bombé et des tempes dégarnies, le regard perçant au fond d'orbites profondes et des sourcils épais, broussailleux, le nez écrasé, la mâchoire carrée. Une ride lui barrait le front comme s'il avait de gros soucis.

2 Il avait une attitude sournoise, une binette pas catholique, un air louche... Je me souviens d'une grosse pomme d'Adam surmontée d'une sale gueule, avec un bec-de-lièvre et des dents cariées!

3 Ce barbu avait une dégaine ordinaire, visage banal, le regard vide et éteint, sans expression, paupières tombantes et poches sous les yeux, un nez en pied de marmite et les lèvres gercées, toutes craquelées. Signe distinctif: il a pris ma montre!

4 Un front haut, protubérant, les yeux en amande, bridés même, endormis, aux pupilles dilatées, narines épatées, nez crochu, cicatrice sur la tempe, oreilles en chou-fleur, joues creuses, dents de lapin, menton fuyant. Si ça peut vous aider, il ressemble à mon cousin, en plus pâle.

5 Plutôt bel homme, du style, de la prestance, avec un nez en trompette, les dents du bonheur, deux belles fossettes, les oreilles délicatement ourlées, et surtout des lèvres charnues, sensuelles, gourmandes. Son visage ouvert, épanoui, m'a fait bonne impression... J'ai noté une lueur de malice dans son regard amusé, avec des pattes d'oie au coin des yeux, quand je lui ai confié mon sac à main.

6 J'en tremble encore de son regard sombre, fuyant, en biais, ses yeux glauques, globuleux, presque exorbités, très cernés, avec de grosses valises, sa bouche édentée, une balafre sur une des bajoues, son cou décharné, flasque, aux chairs molles, pendantes, et cette peau si pâle, translucide, avec les vaisseaux sanguins bien visibles...

7 Il avait d'énormes poches sous les yeux... mais ça, c'est peut-être normal pour un pickpocket...

LUC NISSET.

droopy eyelid
malicious gleam, amused look
crow's-foot
nose like a trumpet
gap teeth
thick, sensuous, sexy lips

translucent skin,
    visible veins
delicately shaped ear
dilated pupil
dilated nostril
smile line
weak chin

eye with rings under it,
    sinister, bulging
    from its socket
bent nose
toothless
chapped, cracked lip

scar on the temple
thick, bushy eyebrow
piercing look
cauliflower ear
smashed-in nose
Adam's apple

high forehead that juts out
wrinkle across the forehead
receding hairline
deep-set eye socket
square jaw
strong bone structure

slanty, almond-
    shaped eye
bags under the
    eyes
hollow cheek
hooked nose

rounded forehead
dark, shifty look
scar
jowl
turkey neck with
    flabby, saggy
    skin

All these needles are most irritating! Are they for learning
a foreign language or for some acupuncture session!

As long as they don't put any weight on me, I'm fine with them!

You run an online dating service, but you're threatened by a class-action lawsuit over false advertising! To ensure the accuracy of the information on your Web site, write new facial descriptions for your clients, based on these photos from their applications.

1. _____ 2. _____ 3. _____

_____ _____ _____

_____ _____ _____

_____ _____ _____

4. _____ 5. _____ 6. _____

_____ _____ _____

_____ _____ _____

_____ _____ _____

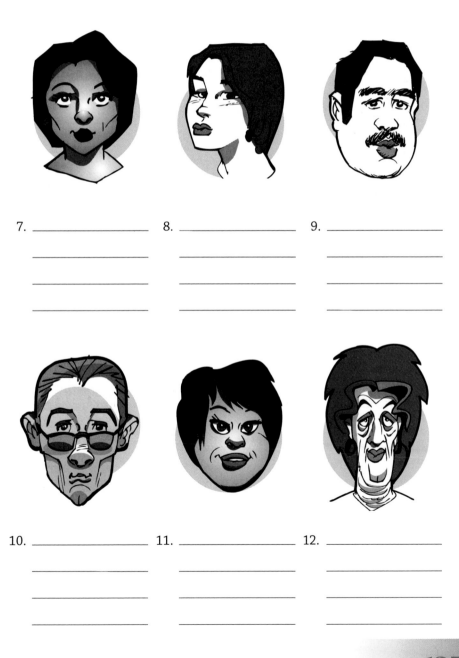

7. _____

_____

_____

_____

8. _____

_____

_____

_____

9. _____

_____

_____

_____

10. _____

_____

_____

_____

11. _____

_____

_____

_____

12. _____

_____

_____

_____

the quarrel

You're always picking a fight with me, looking for trouble!

You get great satisfaction out of fighting!

Get off my back!

If you're looking for trouble, here I am!

T'es toujours à me chercher des crosses, à me chercher noise!

Tu te réalises dans le conflit!

C'est toi qui cherches la merde!

Lâche moi la grappe!

Si tu me cherches tu vas me trouver!

Tu cherches la petite bête dans tout! Tu es mesquin, chipoteur et tatillon!

Je vais finir par en venir aux mains et te casser la gueule!

La bagarre ne me fait pas peur!

You're the one looking for trouble!

You look for faults everywhere. You're petty, you bicker, and you're a nitpicker!

I'll end up getting physical and beat you up!

I'm not afraid to fight!

related terms

agressif(-ive) aggressive
brutal(e) brutal, violent
combatif(-ive) full of fight

querelleur(-euse) quarrelsome
violent(e) violent

affrontement *m* confrontation
bagarre *f* brawl
brouille *f* squabble
conflit *m* conflict
discussion *f* argument
dispute *f* argument

dispute *f* **d'amoureux** lovers' spat
engueulade *f* tiff, row
insultes *fpl* insults
prise *f* **de bec** tussle, argument
reproches *mpl* blame
rupture *f* breakup

La réunion a dégénéré. The meeting got out of hand.

avoir des mots to have an argument
faire une scène to make a scene (public disturbance)
se chamailler to bicker

Ça va mal tourner. This might get bad.
Il y a de la bagarre. There's a fight.
◑ **Tout le monde s'engueule.** Everybody's yelling.

échange *m* **de coups** exchange of blows
échange *m* **verbal** verbal exchange
scène *f* **de ménage** domestic dispute

the raise

J'ai en général l'air renfrogné et la mine chafouine. Aujourd'hui, observez mon visage: je hausse les sourcils, je les fronce, la commissure de mes lèvres tombe, mon regard s'assombrit, se durcit, se noie, se voile. Mon front se plisse. Mes mâchoires se serrent, les veines de mes tempes battent, mes joues se gonflent et se creusent, mes dents grincent et crissent. Mes narines palpitent et se dilatent, je fais la moue. Je roule de gros yeux, ma bouche se tord dans un rictus. Je me mords les lèvres, mon visage est secoué de tics nerveux, les muscles et les veines de mon cou sont tendus à craquer. Mes yeux sont exorbités... Je deviens rubicond... Serait-ce les signes de l'impatience ou d'une simple rage?

I typically look sullen and sly. Look at my face now: I'm raising my eyebrows, I'm frowning, my smile has disappeared, my look has darkened to hard, sunken, and veiled. My brows are knitted. My teeth are clenched, the veins in my temples are pulsing, my cheeks blow in and out, and my teeth are grinding. My nostrils are flaring and I'm grimacing. I'm rolling my eyes and my mouth is tight. I'm biting my lip, my face is shaking with nervous tics, and the muscles and veins in my neck are stretched to the breaking point. My eyes are popping out of their sockets ... I'm turning purple ... Are these signs of impatience or plain old rage?

Heu... Monsieur le Directeur, je propose que nous reparlions de mon augmentation dans un an ou deux, quand vous vous sentirez mieux...

Um ... Boss, how about if we talk about my raise in a couple of years—when you're feeling better?

Stop it, that pisses me off!
That really gets to me!
That gets on my nerves!
I'm gonna explode!
I'm losing my temper!

Enough already! I'm fed up with it!
I've had it up to here ... I'm really fed up!
I've had enough!
It's gone on long enough!
I'm really fed up!

I've told you a hundred times ...
Are you out of your mind?
You've lost your mind!
Are you mocking me?

What a bore!
This guy is boooring!
I'm bored stiff!
Any more boring and you'd die!

Sir, can we have another round?
Another round!
Same accident, same damage!
The same thing!

I'm hungry!
I'm gonna get a snack!
How about a quick snack?
I'm starving!
I've got to get a bite to eat.
Isn't there anything to eat?

No thanks, I'm driving!
I don't drink much.
No alcohol for me!
Just a drop, thanks!
Just a drop!

Something to drink, please!
Can I have a glass, please?
Pour me another one!
I'm so thirsty! I've got to have a drink!

Go to hell!
Up yours!
With all the taxes we pay,
the hell with it!
Fuck you!

Asshole, you want your ass kicked!
You're gonna get a knuckle sandwich,
asshole!
Do you see this fist?

Fuck you, mister!
Go to hell, asshole!
Go screw yourself!

Don't try to con a con man!
DON'T HOLD YOUR BREATH!
Dream on! • Get lost!
I'd like to see it!
Dream on!
That'll be the day!

Eat this!
You're getting a smack in the kisser!
Up your ass!
You asked for it!

You're scared shitless ...
What, are you chickening out?
You're just a chicken, a yellow
belly. You're shitting your pants.
You got no balls!

You're dreaming!
You're pulling my leg!
You take me for some kind of idiot?
I've got my eye on you!
You, wise guy ...

ARE YOU INSANE?
You need help!
Are you nuts or what!
Time for your medicine!
Are you nuts!?
What an asshole!

I'M NOT WORTHY!
I bow down, I worship you!
I'm a huge fan of yours!
MASTER!
I'm your biggest admirer!

SUPER! Very good! My compliments!
BRAVO! Well done! Very good!
Excellent! I love it!
Way to go!

I give you my word of honor!
I swear it!
I swear on my mother's grave (lit., head)!
I've got a reputation to uphold.

You know me!
NEVER IN MY LIFE!
You hear me? NEVER, I would never
have done such a thing!
Cross my heart ...
may I go to hell if I'm lying!

That smells bad!
This guy has terrible breath!
He's got a cadaver behind his teeth!
That stinks / reeks / smells foul!

You're killing me!
How long have we known each other?
WHAT! I must be hallucinating!
Tell me I'm gonna wake up!
How dare you tell me this!
You crack me up!

Wait a minute. Let me think …
You're confusing me.
That stuff is driving me crazy!
True, now that I think about it …

I'm falling asleep standing up.
I'm beat, I'm going to sleep.
I'm gonna hit the sack!
I'm tired. Good night.
I'm dead tired.
I've got to get some sleep.
Tomorrow's another day.
I'm beat!

We'll call each other?
We'll talk soon, okay?
If you don't catch me at home,
try my cell phone!
Give me a ring! • Or call the office!
I don't have a fax.
You've got my e-mail address, right?

SHUT UP!
YADDA YADDA YADDA!
SHUT YOUR BIG MOUTH!
You blabbermouth, shut your pie hole!
Shut your big mouth / trap. /
Shut the hell up!

It's over! It's done! • He's done for!
Keep quiet! Shut up!
(cutting throat) • They went bankrupt!

Wait a minute!
Get me out of this shit!
It's a disaster! • Can you do me a favor?
I'm serious! • I'm in deep shit!

Shhh! Hush up!
Shut your mouth!
Not a sound! Silence!
Be quiet!
You're gonna wake everybody up!
Keep it under your hat!
It's a secret!

Oh my, oh my!
Oh boy!

It's a figure of speech.
Quote ... unquote.
If I may say so ...
You know what I'm trying to say.
You get it. Draw your own conclusion.

Oh that ...
I don't have a clue!
Go figure!
I don't know!
That ...
You ask as if I knew...

Give me 5 minutes!
Coming!
Don't move!
Have you got 2 seconds?

Do you realize what time it is?
I'm so freakin' late! • What time is it?
What time do you have?
Time's a-wastin'! / The clock's ticking!
See you later!

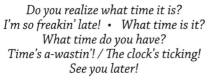

Not a dime in my account!
I don't have a penny to my name!
Flat broke! Busted!
Cleaned out!
I'm destitute!

Very expensive! It costs an arm and a leg!
You're gonna feel the pain buying that!
It's expensive! • It will break us.
It costs an arm and a leg.
You've at least got some cash, huh?
The bill is very steep (lit., salted)!
We can't afford this lifestyle!

I'll drive.
Calm in traffic jams, cool at red lights!
Yes, by car. I've got wheels.
Never a speeding ticket!
I have a car. I can drive for hours.
I'm queen of the road!
When the traffic is light.

Airborne.
I'm going by plane.
As the crow flies.

I prefer to go riding!
Giddyup! In the saddle!
Gallop! Trot!

I'll go on foot!
Walking. On foot!
I'm a pedestrian.
I love going for walks.
A long walk—I love it!

I'm takin' off!
I'm outta here!
I'm gettin' outta here!
I'm splitting!

Plastered!
This guy is seriously drunk!
Totally smashed!
He's dead drunk! Positively sloshed.
A drinking binge, ha!
Three sheets to the wind!
Everybody's off the wagon!

I'm crossing my fingers! Go for it!
Break a leg! (Good luck!)
Step in it, it'll bring you good luck!

I don't give a rat's ass!
I don't give a damn!
Not my problem!
To hell with them!

index